Partnership for the Planet: An Environmental Agenda for the United Nations

HILARY F. FRENCH

Nancy Chege, *Staff Researcher*

Jane A. Peterson, *Editor*

WORLDWATCH PAPER 126
July 1995

THE WORLDWATCH INSTITUTE is an independent, nonprofit environmental research organization in Washington, D.C. Its mission is to foster a sustainable society—in which human needs are met in ways that do not threaten the health of the natural environment or future generations. To this end, the Institute conducts interdisciplinary research on emerging global issues, the results of which are published and disseminated to decisionmakers and the media.

FINANCIAL SUPPORT is provided by the Nathan Cummings Foundation, the Geraldine R. Dodge Foundation, the Energy Foundation, the George Gund Foundation, the Homeland Foundation, the W. Alton Jones Foundation, the John D. and Catherine T. MacArthur Foundation, the Andrew W. Mellon Foundation, the Munson Foundation, the Edward John Noble Foundation, the Pew Charitable Trusts, the Lynn R. and Karl E. Prickett Fund, the Rockefeller Brothers Fund, the Rockefeller Financial Services, the Surdna Foundation, the Turner Foundation, the U.N. Population Fund, the Wallace Genetic Foundation, the Frank Weeden Foundation, and the Winslow Foundation.

PUBLICATIONS of the Institute include the annual *State of the World*, which is now published in 27 languages; *Vital Signs*, an annual compendium of the global trends—environmental, economic, and social—that are shaping our future; the *Environmental Alert* book series; *World Watch* magazine; and the *Worldwatch Papers*. For more information on Worldwatch publications, write: Worldwatch Institute, 1776 Massachusetts Ave., N.W., Washington, DC 20036; or fax 202-296-7365.

THE WORLDWATCH PAPERS provide in-depth, quantitative and qualitative analysis of the major issues affecting prospects for a sustainable society. The Papers are written by members of the Worldwatch Institute research staff and reviewed by experts in the field. Published in five languages, they have been used as a concise and authoritative reference by governments, nongovernmental organizations, and educational institutions worldwide. For a partial list of available Papers, see page 73.

DATA from all graphs and tables contained in this Paper are available on 3 1/2" Macintosh or IBM-compatible computer diskettes. Also includes data from the *State of the World* series, *Vital Signs*, *Environmental Alert* book series, Worldwatch Papers, and *World Watch* magazine. Each yearly subscription includes a mid-year update, and *Vital Signs* and *State of the World* as they are published. The disk is formatted for Lotus 1-2-3, and can be used with Quattro Pro, Excel, SuperCalc, and many other spreadsheets. To order, see page 73.

Table of Contents

Tables and Figures

ACKNOWLEDGMENTS: For their comments on preliminary drafts of this paper, I am grateful to Trigg Talley, Frederik van Bolhuis, and Alexander Wood, as well as to my Worldwatch colleagues Christopher Flavin, Anne Platt, Michael Renner, and Odil Tunali. In addition, I would like to thank Suzanne Clift for her efficient administrative assistance, and the Worldwatch Institute Communication Department for coordinating production and outreach.

HILARY F. FRENCH is a Senior Researcher at Worldwatch Institute, where she studies the connections between environmental issues and international relations. She is the author of five Worldwatch Papers, including Worldwatch Paper 113, *Costly Tradeoffs: Reconciling Trade and the Environment* and Worldwatch Paper 107, *After the Earth Summit: The Future of Environmental Governance.* She is also a co-author of six of the Institute's *State of the World* reports, among other publications.

Introduction

In mid-March 1995, the Canadian Coast Guard fired across the bow of a Spanish trawler on the high seas off the coast of Newfoundland and then seized it on grounds of irresponsible fishing practices—thus escalating one of several major international disputes over depleted fisheries to an unprecedented level of tension. At about the same time, concern that the projected effects of the build-up of greenhouse gases in the atmosphere might already be upon us was heightened by a series of unusual climate-related events in disparate parts of the world: a chunk of Antarctica the size of Rhode Island broke free, and a number of unusually violent storms swept across Europe and other regions. A few months later, in May, an outbreak of the deadly Ebola virus in Zaire added urgency to warnings from the scientific community that humanity could be on the verge of a new era of global epidemics unleashed in part by ecological and social disruption worldwide.[1]

When the United Nations was created a half-century ago, such events would have been difficult to imagine. Environmental degradation was not even considered much of a national threat at that time, let alone a pressing global problem that could provoke international conflict and undermine human health, economic well-being, and social stability. Accordingly, the U.N. Charter does not even mention the word "environment." In 1945, as large parts of Europe and Asia lay in ruins, ensuring that no world war would ever again break out was viewed as the most urgent task before the world community.[2]

At the same time, it was well understood that economic and social cooperation were crucial to human survival: "The battle of peace has to be fought on two fronts," U.S. Secretary of

State Edward Stettinius, Jr., reported back from the San Francisco Conference. "The first is the security front where victory spells freedom from fear. The second is the economic and social front where victory spells freedom from want. Only victory on both fronts can assure the world of an enduring peace." Thus, an active role was foreseen for the U.N. in this economic and social sphere. The "Bretton Woods" institutions—the General Agreement on Tariffs and Trade (GATT), the International Monetary Fund (IMF), and the World Bank—which were established in the forties to focus on management of the global economy, were designated specialized agencies of the U.N., though in practice they have chosen to operate with considerable autonomy.[3]

In the years since the U.N. system was built, environmental security has emerged alongside economic and military security as both a major preoccupation of national decisionmakers and a third pillar of international relations. Several developments account for this shift. One is the magnitude of the problems themselves. Such environmental threats as soil erosion, air and water pollution, overfishing, and water scarcity now cost many countries as much as 5-15 percent of their national income each year, according to the World Bank. What is more, environmental problems often do not respect national borders: wind currents, rainfall, rivers, and streams carry pollutants hundreds or even thousands of miles from their sources. DDT and PCBs, for instance, have been found throughout the Eskimos' food chain in the Arctic, from snow, berries, and fish, to bears. On an even larger scale, the global environmental threats of ozone depletion, climate change, dwindling biological diversity, and ocean pollution threaten all nations.[4]

And the acute suffering inflicted by ecological impoverishment is not always borne in silence. Recent research identifies population growth and resource scarcity as important factors in exacerbating social tensions and even provoking armed conflicts in some regions.[5]

In order to confront proliferating environmental threats, countries have increasingly turned over the last few decades to the United Nations, the one body with the broad mandate and membership required to forge solutions to problems with an impact extending beyond national boundaries. Thus, 50 years after its birth, the U.N. has found a vital new role: protecting and restoring the ecological life support systems on which humanity depends.

Although as early as the 1870s countries occasionally sought to cooperate on issues such as protecting migratory bird species, it was not until a century later that international environmental policy-making began to gather serious momentum. In particular, the 1972 U.N. Conference on the Human Environment in Stockholm marked the arrival of this subject as an international issue. Most notably, the conference created the United Nations Environment Programme (UNEP), which is headquartered in Nairobi and serves as the main focal point for environmental issues within the U.N. system. It also set in motion negotiations toward a number of significant environmental conventions, including the 1972 "London Dumping Convention" on discharging wastes at sea, and the 1973 Convention on International Trade in Endangered Species of Wild Fauna and Flora (CITES).[6]

Since the U.N. system was built, environmental security has emerged as a third pillar of international relations.

The second major milestone in international action on environmental issues was reached in June 1992, when more than a hundred heads of state gathered in Rio de Janeiro for the U.N. Conference on Environment and Development (UNCED). By this time, these issues had become truly global. Unlike many earlier environmental conventions among a small number of neighboring countries, the climate and biological diversity conventions that emerged from the Rio conference cover concerns that are worldwide in scope. If these treaties are to work, they require widespread membership, and indeed both were actually signed by more than one hundred nations in Rio.[7]

By 1992 recognition had grown that protecting the environment requires integrating ecological considerations into social, economic, and foreign policymaking. This integration is central to the concept of "sustainable development," which seeks to meet current human needs while protecting the planet for future generations. The Rio conference marked the coming of age of this critical concept, the point at which it moved from the specialized literature to the front page and into the lexicon of governments and international agencies. In addition to the climate and biological diversity pacts, UNCED produced "Agenda 21," a several hundred-page plan of action for sustainable development, and created the U.N. Commission on Sustainable Development (CSD) to oversee the plan's implementation by international agencies, governments, and civil society worldwide.[8]

Despite all of these efforts, however, the health of the earth's natural systems has declined precipitously in the decades since the United Nations was created, and the pace of the reversal so far shows no signs of letting up. To cite but a few examples, the world's factories, power plants, and automobiles pumped 186 billion tons of carbon into the atmosphere in the years between 1945 and 1995—more than three times as much as was released over all previous centuries. Soil scientists estimate that over this same period either moderate or severe soil erosion affected 1.2 billion hectares—an area equal to the agricultural land of India and China combined. Meanwhile, ecosystems are being disrupted worldwide, fisheries are collapsing, and the earth's forest cover continues to shrink. All of these trends have ominous implications for human welfare, including diminished food for hungry people, drug varieties unavailable to cure cancer, destruction of traditional fishing communities, and the disappearance of numerous island countries that are literally threatened with drowning in the rising seas resulting from global warming.[9]

The growing discrepancy between apparent success as measured by the increasing number of international environmental treaties and other agreements and the deteriorating state of the biosphere itself stems from a number of factors. One is the wide gap between official rhetoric and actual implementation. In reality, many treaties contain few real commitments, and even those that are in place are not always translated into action.

Moreover, the world's richer countries have not made sufficient resources available to the world's poorer countries to help them meet the terms of existing accords.[10]

Another impediment to the environmental work of different international institutions is the overlap among them, which causes widespread confusion about their respective roles. U.N. agencies such as the Commission on Sustainable Development, the United Nations Development Programme (UNDP), and UNEP are all actively involved in the effort to promote sustainable development. The World Bank, the International Monetary Fund, and the new World Trade Organization (WTO) are also influential actors, as is the Global Environment Facility (GEF)— a joint undertaking of UNDP, UNEP, and the World Bank designed to finance projects that will benefit the global environment. Rationalizing and streamlining this scattered array of activities would help the United Nations lay down a sustainable path to the future.

Despite all these efforts, the health of the earth's natural systems has declined precipitously.

As the world celebrates the 50th anniversary of the U.N.'s birth, a sober assessment is needed of whether or not yesterday's institutions are adequately equipped to confront the transnational problems of the present, let alone the future. In the environmental arena, the answer is clearly no. At the same time, the need to protect the earth's natural resources ranks high on the list of reasons the world will require stronger and more effective international institutions in the years ahead. Thus it is time to launch a far-reaching process of reform equipping the United Nations to mobilize the international effort required to ensure that today's children can thrive without endangering prospects for their descendants.

Treaties for the Earth

Just over a quarter century ago, photographs of the earth taken from space by the Apollo expeditions helped launch the modern environmental movement, indelibly impressing on all who saw them that this planet, while divided by political boundaries, is united by ecological systems. Inspired by this vision, the world has made considerable progress in the years since in developing international rules aimed at cooperatively managing shared resources—especially the oceans, the atmosphere, and biological diversity.[11]

Hundreds of agreements, declarations, action plans, and international treaties on the environment have now been negotiated covering such shared concerns as acid rain contamination, ocean pollution, endangered species protection, hazardous waste trade, and the preservation of Antarctica—many of them under U.N. auspices. Environmental treaties alone now number more than 170, and agreement on more than two-thirds of them has been reached since the Stockholm conference in 1972. (See Figure 1.) If other, less-binding types of accords are included in the total, the number of international environmental instruments tops 800.[12]

Some of these agreements have only amounted to words, but many have led to measurable actions, proving that when the conditions are ripe, international collaboration can work. Air pollution in Europe, for instance, has been reduced dramatically as a result of the 1979 treaty on transboundary air pollution. Global chlorofluorocarbon (CFC) emissions have dropped 77 percent from their peak in 1988 as a result of the 1987 Montreal Protocol on ozone depletion and its subsequent amendments. The killing of elephants has plummeted in Africa since the 1990 ban on commercial trade in ivory under the Convention on International Trade in Endangered Species of Wild Flora and Fauna. And mining exploration and development have been forbidden in Antarctica for 50 years under a 1991 accord. It does not minimize the achievement these accords represent to say that now more aggressive action is needed to strengthen and implement existing agreements if they are to succeed in restoring the health of critical ecological systems before the damage becomes irreversible.[13]

The vast majority of environmental agreements are bilateral or regional in scope, involving, for instance, the manage-

FIGURE 1

International Environmental Treaties, 1920–1995 (cumulative)

Number of Treaties

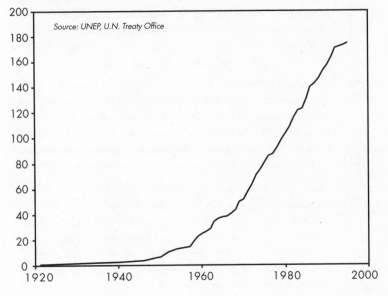

Source: UNEP, U.N. Treaty Office

ment of river systems, air corridors, or migratory bird species. However, a minority of environmental issues—including the atmosphere, international waterways, and biological diversity—are truly global. The last few decades have seen steady progress toward developing international rules governing these "global commons." (See Table 1.)[14]

The oceans were the first such commons to become the subject of intensive international deliberations. After 10 years of difficult negotiations, governments from around the world gathered at the United Nations in New York to adopt the Law of the Sea Convention in 1982. However, it was not until 12 years later, in 1994, that this convention finally received the 60 ratifications required for it to enter into force. Significantly, agreement was also reached that year on modifications to the controversial seabed mining provisions of the original document that were intended to satisfy some long-held concerns of the United States

TABLE 1

A Timeline of Selected International Environmental Agreements[1]

1946   **International Whaling Convention.** 50 parties.
        Protects whales from excessive harvesting. Amended in 1982
        to ban all commercial whaling. Whale harvests fell from
        38,977 in 1970 to 726 in 1993 as a result.

1959   **Antarctica Treaty.** 42 parties. Subjects continent to joint
        management by original 12 parties and others who conduct
        scientific research there "in the interests of all mankind."
        Protocol signed in 1991 bans mining exploration and develop-
        ment for 50 years, protects wildlife, regulates waste disposal
        and marine pollution, and provides for scientific monitoring of
        the continent.

1972   **London Dumping Convention.** 75 parties. Initially
        banned dumping of high-level radioactive and highly toxic
        wastes at sea. Ban on dumping of low-level radioactive
        wastes and on ocean incineration of wastes in effect since
        1994. At the end of 1995, dumping of all forms of industrial
        wastes will be outlawed.

1973   **Washington Convention on International Trade in
        Endangered Species of Wild Fauna and Flora
        (CITES).** 128 parties. Restricts trade in species that are either
        threatened with extinction or may become endangered if their
        trade is not regulated. Ban on trade in ivory imposed in
        1990. Killing of elephants declined dramatically as a result.

1973   **MARPOL.** 95 parties. Restricts intentional discharges by
        ships, such as oil and sewage. Amended in 1978 and again
        in 1992. MARPOL has been most effective in limiting dis-
        charges near shore.

1982   **Convention on the Law of the Sea.** 75 parties. An
        umbrella agreement. Establishes 200-mile "exclusive econom-
        ic zones." Also includes provisions on conservation of living
        resources of the oceans, maintenance and restoration of popu-
        lations of species, and protection of the sea from pollution.

TABLE 1, CONTINUED

1987   **Montreal Protocol on Substances that Deplete the
        Ozone Layer.** 149 parties. (London Amendments in 1990,
        and Copenhagen Amendments in 1992.) With amendments,
        requires phase-out of CFCs in industrial countries by 1996
        and imposes restrictions on the use of a number of other
        ozone-depleting chemicals. CFC emissions down 77 percent
        since 1988 as a result.

1989   **Basel Convention.** 88 parties. Controls the transbound-
        ary movement of hazardous wastes. Updated in 1993 to
        completely ban exports to non-OECD countries by 1988.

1992   **Framework Convention on Climate Change.** 136
        parties. Includes target for industrial countries of stabilizing
        carbon dioxide levels at 1990 levels by the year 2000.
        Requires developing countries to undertake emissions invento-
        ries and other studies. Negotiations now under way to
        strengthen commitments in order to meet the treaty's goal of
        stabilizing the overall concentration of carbon dioxide in the
        atmosphere.

1992   **Convention on Biological Diversity.** 118 parties.
        Establishes broad framework for the conservation of biologi-
        cal diversity, the sustainable use of its components, and the
        fair and equitable sharing of the benefits arising out of the use
        of genetic resources.

1994   **Convention on Desertification.** 106 signatories and one
        party. Combats desertification by implementing strategies
        focused on sustainable management of land and water.
        Supplies framework for local projects; encourages national
        action programs; establishes mechanism to coordinate funds;
        encourages trust funds.

---

[1]Where no results are listed, it is because they are not quantifiable or are as yet
unavailable.

Source: Worldwatch Institute, based on sources documented in endnote 14.

and other industrial countries, thereby hopefully paving the way for them to join in. Australia, Germany, and Italy are among those that have now done so, but it remains to be seen if the accord will receive approval from the United States Senate.[15]

The recent rebirth of the Law of the Sea treaty comes just in time for the world's oceans and estuaries, which are suffering from overfishing, oil spills, land-based sources of pollution such as sewage and pesticide run-off, and other assaults. The primary motivations for the treaty were originally economic and strategic: to establish countries' rights to a 200-mile economic zone (called exclusive economic zone, or EEZ) off their coasts while still ensuring freedom of navigation. But the Law of the Sea also contains some important environmental provisions. For instance, though countries are granted sovereignty and economic rights over waters within 200 miles of their shores, they also accept an obligation to protect ecological health there. In addition, the accord serves as an umbrella for scores of existing international agreements covering the oceans, including the London Dumping Convention, the MARPOL treaty regulating shipping, and numerous international fisheries agreements and regionally based initiatives. All signatories of the Law of the Sea are obligated to adhere to these various conventions. And many—though not all—of the environmental provisions in the accord are subject to the treaty's pathbreaking compulsory dispute resolution provisions, which bind countries to accept the verdict of an international tribunal.[16]

In the years since the Law of the Sea agreement was first struck, most of its provisions—including the environmental ones—have been widely accepted around the world as "customary" international law. The entry into force of the convention will make obligations accepted in the accord legally binding on its members, and violations of them will become subject to enforcement procedures. Although these are important advances, the real work of ensuring the ocean's health has only just begun. The convention is a useful framework that urgently needs to be strengthened and built upon. For instance, issues such as land-based sources of pollution and the destruction of coastal habitat, including mangrove swamps and salt flats, remain to be adequately addressed.[17]

To date, the primary international response to these coastal issues has come through UNEP's Regional Seas Program, which has developed regionally based action plans for 12 such seas. Several of these programs have led to binding accords, sometimes among traditional political adversaries. For instance, the action plan for the Mediterranean Sea counts among its members Syria, Israel, and Lebanon. With the program, a non-binding agreement forms the umbrella under which stronger commitments are subsequently hammered out, as in the convention covering land-based sources of pollution reached in 1980 by parties to the first regional seas program, the Mediterranean Action Plan.

Despite initial successes, in all of the regions much work remains to be done to turn non-binding statements of good intentions into concrete measures. Scarcities of funding for implementation of existing agreements have been a particular problem. Meanwhile, UNEP has convened talks aimed at developing a Global Program of Action for protection of the marine environment. A number of land-based compounds including persistent organic compounds, will be addressed. The action plan is expected to be finalized at an international meeting to be held in Washington, D.C., in late October 1995.[18]

Scarcities of funding for implementation of agreements have been a particular problem.

The crisis in the world's fisheries provides the most dramatic example of the shortcomings in the current system of international oceans governance. According to the U.N. Food and Agriculture Organization (FAO), all 15 of the world's major fishing grounds are now at or beyond their sustainable limits. At the June 1992 Earth Summit, governments agreed to conduct a series of negotiations at the United Nations to discuss possible international action to remedy this situation. They agreed to focus primarily on the matter of fish stocks that straddle the boundaries of economic zones and of fish species that migrate long distances—problems that the Law of the Sea failed to resolve.[19]

The negotiations have proven difficult, with starkly different interests emerging between coastal states, such as Canada, which worry about the actions of foreign fishers in international waters adjacent to their own, and those with long-distance fishing fleets, such as Spain, which focus more on the failure of coastal states to adequately protect fisheries within their waters. Nevertheless, the dramatic confrontation between these two countries galvanized the international talks, and the bilateral agreement struck between them is now being looked to as the model for a binding multilateral treaty now under negotiation. Notably, the treaty is expected to endorse a precautionary approach to the management of fish stocks. Violations of the accord will be subject to compulsory dispute resolution. Enforcement procedures are still under discussion, but could include innovative provisions for boarding vessels in international waters for monitoring purposes.[20]

The second major attempt to develop a management system for a globally shared commons was also the most successful to date: the effort to restore the ozone layer in the stratosphere, which protects the earth and its inhabitants from ultraviolet radiation. In the mid-seventies, scientists first began to theorize that widely used chlorine-containing industrial chemicals known as CFCs, as well as those containing bromines, might be causing chemical reactions in the stratosphere that were ravaging the ozone layer, thereby allowing excessive levels of ultraviolet radiation to reach Earth. The United Nations Environment Programme launched international cooperative research efforts that led, in March 1985, to the Vienna Convention, a framework treaty providing for continued research and setting in motion negotiations aimed at controlling substances harmful to the ozone layer. As in the fishing case, rapid international action was then spurred by a crisis: the world was shocked in May 1985 by the discovery of an "ozone hole" over Antarctica so big that some believed it could be seen from as far away as Mars.[21]

Just over two years later, in September 1987, the historic Montreal Protocol on the Depletion of the Ozone Layer was signed, initially by 26 countries. The protocol called for industrial nations to cut production of CFCs in half by 1999, and for emissions of halons to be frozen at 1986 levels by 1992. Strengthened significantly two times since then, the protocol now stipulates that the production of CFCs in industrial countries must be phased out altogether by 1996. It also restricts the use of several other ozone-depleting chemicals, including halons, carbon tetrachlorides, methyl bromide, methyl chloroform, and hydrochlorofluorocarbons. Treaty members are currently considering further restrictions on some of these chemicals. Developing countries have a 10-year grace period in which to meet the terms of the original protocol and its amendments.[22]

In a remarkably short period of time, the Montreal Protocol has been translated into changes in domestic policies around the world. More than a hundred countries have ratified the original agreement, and both amendments have received enough approvals to enter into force. Once CFC manufacturers recognized that the handwriting was on the wall, they moved aggressively and successfully to develop substitute chemicals. Given the quick and dramatic reduction in CFC emissions resulting from the pact, computer models suggest that if all countries comply with their commitments, chlorine concentrations in the lower atmosphere will begin to level off soon and the ozone layer will begin to recover. (See Figure 2.) Although this would be a momentous international achievement, the world would nevertheless have paid a heavy price for earlier inaction. Even assuming full compliance with the accord, excessive levels of ultraviolet radiation will be reaching the earth for the next half-century and, according to scientists' estimates, will continue to stunt agricultural productivity and damage ecological and human health.[23]

The lessons learned in the ozone treaty are now being put to a severe test as the international community begins to confront a more daunting challenge related to the atmosphere—the need to head off climate change. In March 1994, less than two years after it was signed in Rio, the Framework Convention on Climate Change entered into force once the 50th country (Portugal) ratified it. As of June 1995, a total of 136 nations had become par-

The Impact of the Montreal Protocol and Its Amendments on Atmospheric Chlorine Concentrations, 1975–2055

Parts per Billion by Volume

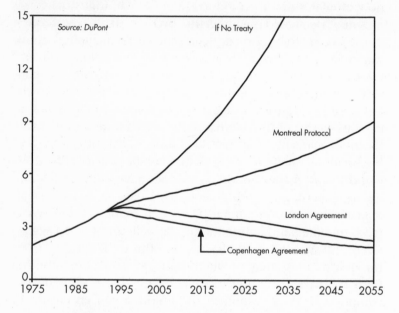

ties. Unfortunately, the speed with which the treaty was ratified was in part a reflection of the fact that it currently contains few real commitments.[24]

The climate treaty's deliberately ambiguous language so far only urges, but does not require, industrial nations to hold total emissions of greenhouse gases to 1990 levels or less by the year 2000. Developing nations face no numerical goals yet, though all signatories must conduct inventories of their emissions; submit detailed reports of national actions taken to implement the convention; and endeavor to take climate change into account in all their social, economic, and environmental policies.[25]

As of late 1994, most industrial countries had established national greenhouse gas targets and climate plans, but they vary widely in effectiveness. Among the few ambitious and comprehensive plans are those of Denmark, The Netherlands, and Switzerland, where oil and coal industries are less powerful political forces than elsewhere. Through the use of efficiency standards, renewable energy programs, and carbon taxes, these plans are likely to limit national emissions significantly.[26]

However, independent evaluations indicate that most of the climate plans issued so far will do relatively little to slow greenhouse gas emissions. This is because they consist mainly of modest, voluntary policies. A series of long-standing efforts by the European Union to impose a hybrid carbon/energy tax have so far failed, despite strong support from the European Commission, while the United States has been unable to raise its gasoline taxes, which, at one-fifth the European level, are among the world's lowest. Although the United Kingdom, Germany, Russia, and Ukraine are all likely to meet the treaty's year 2000 emissions goal, this is mainly a result of actions and developments unrelated to their national climate plans: the reduction of coal subsidies in the United Kingdom and the shutdown of energy-intensive heavy industries in eastern Germany and the former Soviet Union. Meanwhile, some of the world's heaviest carbon emitters, including Australia, Canada, and the United States, are continuing to *increase* their emissions steadily, and are likely to reach at least 5 percent over 1990 emission levels in 2000.[27]

Most of the climate plans issued so far will do little to slow greenhouse gas emissions.

Even if the goal of holding emissions to 1990 levels in 2000 is met, further efforts will be needed to achieve the broader aim of the Rio climate treaty, which is to stabilize atmospheric concentrations of greenhouse gases. Doing so will require bringing carbon emissions 60-80 percent below current levels, according to scientists. With this reality in mind, the initial Conference of the Parties to the convention met in Berlin in March 1995 to consider whether and how to update the treaty. A caucus of vulnerable small island states and environmental groups had urged this meeting to adopt a target of a 20 percent cut in carbon emissions by 2005. Although such stringent goals did not find

immediate support, governments did consent to initiate negotiations aimed at agreeing within two years on targets for emissions levels after 2000 for industrial countries, about which the
current treaty is noticeably silent. They also decided to discuss
joint actions that might help achieve these goals, such as revamp-
ing energy, forest, and transport policies. Finally, industrial countries launched a series of "joint implementation" pilot projects
designed to encourage investments in developing countries
directed into less carbon-intensive energy technologies and into
planting trees to sequester carbon.[28]

Work is also slowly getting under way to implement the
other major treaty agreed to in Rio—the Convention on
Biological Diversity. Signed by 160 countries, this treaty entered
into force on December 29, 1993. As of June 1995, a total of 118
countries had ratified it, including many in both the North and
the South. The first Conference of the Parties to the convention
was held late in 1994 in Nassau, the Bahamas. One country was
notably absent as an official party, however—the United States.
The agreement encountered rough sailing when it was considered by the U.S. Senate in 1994 and has yet to be ratified.[29]

As with protecting the atmosphere, preserving biological
diversity is something that all countries have a stake in and
that no one country can effectively do alone. Ironically, however, one of the convention's most important achievements
was its rejection of the notion that biological diversity is the
"common heritage of mankind," accompanied—conversely—by
its recognition that biological resources are the sovereign property of nation states. Although international pharmaceutical
companies have been extracting genes from countries for free for
years, the biological diversity convention says that gene-rich
nations have a right to charge for access to this valuable resource,
and it allows them to pass national legislation to set the terms.
The hope is that if these countries view their genetic resources
as a source of potential profits, they will have a strong incentive
to preserve them.[30]

The protection from pests, diseases, and climatic and soil vari-
ations that genetic variability affords crops is worth some $1 bil-
lion to U.S. agriculture. Overall, the economic benefits that

the pharmaceutical, agricultural, forest-product, fishing, and chemical industries receive from wild species add up to more than $87 billion annually in the United States—over 4 percent of the gross domestic product.[31]

One promising model of a way to use biodiversity's economic value as a conservation tool is a 1991 agreement between Merck & Co., the world's largest pharmaceutical company, and Costa Rica's National Institute of Biodiversity (INBio). Merck agreed to pay the institute $1 million for conservation programs in exchange for access to the country's plants, microbes, and insects. And should a discovery make its way into a commercialized product, Merck will pay INBio a share of the royalties. Discussing how to replicate such agreements on a large scale will likely be a high priority for countries that have signed the convention.[32]

Preserving biological diversity is something that all countries have a stake in.

Besides providing a forum for future negotiations, the convention calls for a number of actions by governments to preserve biological wealth, including national plans and strategies for preservation and detailed biological inventories and surveys. Work on strategies has begun in a number of countries, including Canada, Chile, Indonesia, The Netherlands, Norway, Poland, and the United Kingdom; the United States and Costa Rica are currently in the process of conducting biological surveys.[33]

Although these actions represent important first steps, much work remains to be done to build upon the biodiversity treaty. The 1992 accord largely represented a framework for future actions, rather than the end of the process, and now it needs to be filled in. Given the speed with which species are being lost around the world, quick action is essential. A first step in this direction was taken by the Nassau meeting, which agreed to a work plan for the next two years that, among other things, includes discussions on coastal and marine biodiversity and intellectual property rights issues, as well as consideration of a possible protocol on biotechnology safety.[34]

Making Environmental Treaties Work

Reaching agreement on a treaty is of course only the first step. Then the real work begins of continuing to update it in light of new scientific information or changing political circumstances, and of ensuring that paper commitments are translated into real policy changes in countries around the world. For the major international environmental conventions, these tasks largely fall to two categories of institutions: the secretariats and other bodies set up under the framework of the treaties themselves, and funding sources—most prominently the Global Environment Facility.

At a minimum, each individual treaty spawns a Conference of the Parties and a secretariat. Conferences of the Parties are regular meetings of treaty members, which provide an opportunity to strengthen the agreement and review problems in implementation. Secretariats are the small offices set up to service these meetings of governments.

Though secretariats play a potentially important role in overseeing the implementation of accords, all too often governments vest them with limited resources and authority. For instance, they generally do not have the wherewithal or authority to verify the information governments are supposed to supply on implementation efforts. A typical secretariat employs fewer than 20 staff members and has an annual budget of $1-3 million, a drop in the bucket compared to the budgets of U.S. federal agencies charged with implementing domestic environmental laws.[35]

A notable exception is the CITES (endangered species) secretariat, which has been granted considerable powers by governments and has used them to positive effect. It possesses, for example, the power to demand explanations from countries it believes are falling short of meeting treaty obligations. However, limited resources have prevented the secretariat from making full use of its authority.[36]

Governments, for their part, often fail to provide secretariats with complete and timely information as required. A 1992 study by the U.S. General Accounting Office found that, while 80 percent of the parties to the Montreal Protocol had presented the required reports, only 30 percent of the members of the London Dumping Convention, and less than a quarter of the CITES parties, had done so.[37]

The scattered locations of secretariats about the globe pose a further problem. For instance, the secretariat for the ozone treaty sits in Nairobi; the climate change treaty's office will be located in Bonn; and that of the biodiversity treaty will likely be housed in either Kenya, Spain, or Switzerland. UNEP has been granted control over some of these administrative groups; others report to different U.N. agencies. Centralizing these bodies under one roof would offer opportunities for the exchange of information and ideas, thereby making international environmental governance a more efficient process. Governments cautiously endorsed the idea of centrally locating convention secretariats in Agenda 21, but in practice they have been reluctant to follow through on this idea. Although a small amount of consolidation has taken place in Geneva, further efforts in this direction have run afoul of the desires of individual countries to house these offices in order to enhance their own prestige.[38]

As is true with any treaty, a key challenge for making environmental agreements work is ensuring that their provisions are actually implemented. Although reporting requirements are one means toward this end, in some cases actual penalties such as fines or trade sanctions are called for.

The use of trade restrictions to encourage countries to participate in a treaty or to punish violators has proven particularly controversial. Such sanctions have been used effectively in the case of both CITES and the Montreal Protocol. For instance, in 1991 parties to CITES restricted trade in wildlife products with Thailand because of reports that it was a center of illegal wildlife trade. As a result, Thailand clamped down on this activity. Under the Montreal Protocol, parties are forbidden from trading in CFCs or products containing them with countries that are not members of the treaty. These provisions were designed to ensure that CFC production was not simply transferred to non-parties. In both cases, the use of trade measures is critical to the success of the treaty. However, it is unclear whether or not current world trade rules permit the practice. The Committee on Trade and

Environment at the World Trade Organization, which recently supplanted the GATT, is studying this question.[39]

Although the punitive approach embodied by penalties and sanctions has its place, it is not always appropriate or effective. Shortages of financial and technological resources, more than a lack of will, render many developing countries unable to comply with some treaty requirements. Thus, a more critical issue for the success or failure of most treaties is whether or not adequate funding is made available to help developing countries make the investments required to meet their terms. The ozone treaty was the first environmental accord to create a sizable fund for this purpose. At a June 1990 meeting, governments agreed to create a $240 million fund for 1991-93; an additional $455 million was pledged in 1992 for 1994-96. The creation of this facility was pivotal in convincing developing countries such as China and India to sign the treaty. Had they not done so, emissions gains from non-participants could have overwhelmed emissions reductions in signatory countries, undermining the effectiveness of the accord.[40]

Unfortunately, the ozone fund has been beset by a number of problems in its implementation. One has been delinquent payments by donor nations: it is currently suffering from a shortfall of $217 million in monies promised by governments but not yet received. Another involves delays in executing projects by the implementing agencies, which include UNDP, UNEP, the U.N. Industrial Development Organization (UNIDO), and the World Bank. Despite these shortcomings, the fund has now launched programs aimed at phasing out the use of ozone-depleting substances in 70 countries. Projects now in progress are expected to eliminate some 50,000 tons of these substances. There is little time to lose in implementing these plans: only if countries meet commitments they have made under the Montreal Protocol and its amendments will the ozone layer begin to recover as projected by scientists.[41]

With the ozone fund model in mind, countries created the Global Environment Facility in 1991 to finance investments in preserving the global commons—the atmosphere, biological diversity, and international waterways. Donors committed an initial $1.3 billion in funds to be spent over a three-year pilot phase to reimburse recipient countries for any "incremental"—or extra—costs they might incur as a result of efforts to protect these shared resources. After Rio, the GEF was designated as the "interim funding mechanism" for the climate and biodiversity treaties—a status that has been reaffirmed at the recent Conferences of the Parties to these conventions. In March 1994, after months of arduous negotiations, governments agreed to make the GEF permanent and to replenish it with $2 billion in new resources to be spent over the next three years. As of April 1995, the facility had allocated $766 million in grants—46 percent for biological diversity preservation, 35 percent for climate-related initiatives, 15 percent to protect international waters, 3 percent for overarching projects, and 1 percent for projects aimed at heading off ozone depletion.[42]

Only if countries meet commitments they have made under the Montreal Protocol will the ozone layer begin to recover.

At the time the GEF was first created in 1991, governments did not want to create a new international institution. Instead, they decided to make the GEF a joint undertaking of UNDP, UNEP, and the World Bank. UNDP was charged with carrying out technical assistance and capacity-building projects and with implementing a program of small grants to non-governmental organizations (NGOs); UNEP was given the role of providing scientific and technical advice—particularly as to the soundness of GEF initiatives; and the World Bank was made responsible for investment projects, as well as for managing GEF funds and administering the facility.[43]

The GEF proved controversial in its pilot phase. For one thing, its close association with the Bank was a source of concern both to developing countries, which resented the fact that donor states have disproportionate clout there, and to many NGOs, whose long experience with the Bank had made them skeptical of its suitability for the job—particularly given its tradition of keeping critical information secret and not consulting adequately with the citizens who are directly affected by its projects.

An independent evaluation of GEF called for by its member governments in the course of the replenishment negotiations confirmed that there had been major flaws both in the concept underlying the pilot phase and in its execution. It concluded that fundamental changes were needed in GEF strategies and functions, in the relationships between the three agencies involved, and in the facility's operating procedures.[44]

As a result of these criticisms, several changes were made under the 1994 replenishment agreement to the way the GEF is governed. For instance, it was consciously made more independent from the World Bank than it had been during its pilot phase. Toward this end, an independent GEF secretariat was created along with a governing council that will exercise control over the project approval process. In addition, a new and innovative "double majority" voting system was devised for this body. Decisions will normally be made by consensus. But in cases where this proves impossible and a matter is put to a vote, two consecutive tallies will be required—the first on the basis of a one-nation, one-vote system similar to that used at the United Nations, and the second by a one-dollar, one-vote system comparable to that of the Bretton Woods institutions. This voting arrangement is intended to make the facility a truly joint undertaking of donors and recipients—an innovative notion that may offer a useful precedent for the governance of other international institutions.[45]

More than a year after the new GEF began operations, the jury is still out as to how well the reforms are working. The GEF secretariat is currently developing a concept paper for the governing council's consideration that will guide its investments. It is also writing policies covering critical issues such as the project preparation process and procedures for consulting with local peoples affected by GEF projects.[46]

Significantly, member governments are reviewing the manner in which the GEF applies the controversial concept of incremental costs. The facility's mandate to finance the extra costs to countries of investing in projects of global benefit frustrates recipient countries, which resent the fact that donor states appear more concerned about responding to abstract global threats than about addressing urgent local environmental needs.

The incremental cost concept can also foster the false notion that activities such as preserving biological diversity, investing in renewable energy, and preventing coastal pollution are not worth pursuing out of national and local self-interest alone. To avoid the danger of its serving as a disincentive for investing in projects that offer global and local benefits at the same time, the calculation of incremental costs is best viewed as a loose guiding concept rather than as a precise operational procedure in the implementation of GEF projects.[47]

Given its limited resources, the key question for the GEF is how it can leverage them into broader efforts to reorient both national policies and other international financial flows in support of development strategies that do not undermine the integrity of global systems. The GEF could help spur this broader action in a number of ways. One is by cooperating with its three implementing agencies to provide recipient countries with advice on how to design global-commons-friendly policies. For instance, financing the preparation of a study that reveals opportunities for cost-effective investments in renewable energy might yield far greater carbon reduction benefits over the long run than money spent on bankrolling any particular plant. The GEF can also play a catalyzing role by cooperating through co-financing arrangements with other organizations, including the International Development Association (the World Bank's soft-loan arm) and the International Finance Corporation (IFC, the Bank's private sector arm).[48]

The jury is still out as to how well the GEF reforms are working.

One continuing source of tension in the effort to devise effective policies for protecting the global commons is the at times conflicting advice emerging from the Conferences of the Parties to the conventions and from the GEF's governing council. Often, national government delegations to these proceedings are composed of representatives of different agencies with different agendas. Thus the environment minister might deliver one message to the Conference of Parties, to be contradicted directly by the same country's finance minister at the GEF

Council meeting. Complicating matters further is the GEF's continued status as the provisional, as opposed to permanent, funding arm of the conventions—largely a result of ongoing developing-country distrust of the GEF. Better coordination among different agencies at the national level both in donor and recipient countries would help ensure that mixed messages do not result in policy paralysis—while the state of the global environment continues to deteriorate.

Sorting Out the Roles of U.N. Bodies

Considerable confusion exists about the respective roles of the various U.N. bodies involved with environmental issues—including the United Nations Environment Programme, the Commission on Sustainable Development, the United Nations Development Programme, and many U.N. specialized agencies. In large measure, the confusion stems from one of the main conundrums of sustainable development: the need to ensure that environmental considerations are integrated into broader economic and development policies. Because this integration is essential, protecting the environment cannot be viewed as the sole domain of a U.N. environmental authority. But in diffusing ecological responsibilities broadly throughout the U.N. system, there is a danger that these issues will be buried amid competing and sometimes contradictory concerns. Clarifying the roles of the many different players is essential if the United Nations is to be able to fulfill its mission of heading off ecological decline around the world.

To understand the current confused state of the U.N.'s response to environmental imperatives, it is helpful to consider some history. When UNEP was created in 1972, the important role that independent environmental agencies play at the national level had yet to be demonstrated. Governments worried that the creation of a U.N. environment agency might take pressure off other U.N. agencies such as the Food and Agriculture Organization and the World Health Organization (WHO) to integrate environmental considerations into their programs. Thus, UNEP was given the role of catalyzing environmental activities throughout the U.N. system. Because it was not to engage in projects of its own, governments decreed that UNEP's staff was to be small. The UNEP architects created an "environment fund" as the main tool through which the agency was to exercise its influence in the U.N. system; it was to control pursestrings that other agencies could access for environmental programs.[49]

However, governments failed to deliver on their promises of significant resources for the environment fund. In its first two decades, UNEP's total resources amounted to less than $1 billion. Indeed, total spending over its lifetime is less than UNDP's annual budget. UNEP's budget today of just over $100 million a year is comparable to the budgets of some private environmental groups and significantly smaller than those of most other U.N. agencies. (See Table 2.)[50]

Another problem is UNEP's location in Nairobi, far from the other U.N. agencies it is theoretically coordinating. "In the context of the U.N. system, with its focus on New York and Geneva, the decision to locate UNEP in Nairobi was also an expression of disdain for its mission," notes Konrad von Moltke of Dartmouth College and the World Wildlife Fund. "A major, independent organization would have had extraordinary difficulties being located far from the decision-making centers of the U.N. system. It was all but inconceivable that an agency with a 'catalytic' mission could function in a remote location."[51]

Despite these handicaps, UNEP has had its share of successes in its first 20 years. For instance, it launched the Global Environment Monitoring System in 1975, which collects a variety of important information, including data on climatic trends such as the advance and decline of glaciers and air and water pollution levels in cities around the world. UNEP has also played a central role in the negotiation of numerous environmental action plans and treaties, including the regional seas program and the ozone treaty. Its Industry and Environment office, located in Paris, has been an important source of technical advice on waste-minimizing technologies and on the prevention of industrial accidents. Elizabeth Dowdeswell, who has headed UNEP since 1993, has recently taken a number of positive steps to make the organization a more significant force. For instance,

TABLE 2

Estimated Expenditures and Staffing of Various U.N. Agencies, 1992 and 1993[1]

Agency	Professional Staff	Expenditure
	(number)	(million dollars)
U.N. Development Programme (UNDP)	1,571	2,235
U.N. Children's Fund (UNICEF)	1,179	1,810
Food and Agriculture Org. (FAO)	2,659	1,557
World Health Org. (WHO)	1,833	1,372
International Labour Org. (ILO)	1,373	676
U.N. Education, Scientific and Cultural Org. (UNESCO)	1,056	662
Int'l. Atomic Energy Agency (IAEA)	699	535
U.N. Industrial Development Org. (UNIDO)	660	491
U.N. Population Fund (UNFPA)	166	333
U.N. Environment Programme (UNEP)	303	214
World Meteorological Org. (WMO)	182	145
International Maritime Org. (IMO)	122	82

[1]Budget figures are for the two-year period covering 1992 and 1993 but staff size figures are for 1990 except for UNEP (1993) and UNFPA (1994).

Sources: Budget figures from United Nations, "Programs and resources of the United Nations system for the biennium 1992-1993," Report of the Administrative Committee on Coordination, Economic and Social Council, Geneva, June 10, 1993; staff sizes from Erskine Childers with Brian Urquhart, *Renewing the United Nations System* (Uppsala, Sweden: Dag Hammarskjöld Foundation, 1994), except for UNFPA staff size from Bikash Shrestha, UNFPA, New York, private communication, October 18, 1994, and UNEP budget and staff size from Sergei Khromov, UNEP, Nairobi, private communication, October 31, 1994.

its regional offices have been strengthened, including one at U.N. headquarters in New York, one in Geneva, and one in Bangkok.[52]

Meanwhile, however, other U.N. institutions have emerged as important environmental players, raising questions about

UNEP's role. At the Earth Summit in 1992, governments created two new bodies whose missions overlap with UNEP's mandate. Most importantly, the Commission on Sustainable
Development was created to provide a forum where governments could review progress in implementing Agenda 21, share
information about what works and what does not, and discuss
impediments such as inadequate financial resources or lack of
access to innovative technologies. The CSD was given the task
of monitoring the activities of national governments, international organizations, and private actors.
Because Agenda 21 covers almost all **Governments**
environment and development issues, **failed to deliver**
the CSD's mandate is far-reaching.[53] **on their promises**

To work parallel to the CSD, gov- **of significant**
ernments at Rio also created an Inter- **resources for**
Agency Committee on Sustainable
Development (IACSD) composed of
representatives of several relevant U.N. **UNEP's**
agencies to try to improve coordina- **environment**
tion and cooperation between them. **fund.**
In addition, an organizational shake-up
at the U.N. Secretariat in New York
resulted in the establishment of a new Department for Policy
Coordination and Sustainable Development, headed by Under-
Secretary-General Nitin Desai. Among its vast array of responsibilities, this office provides staff support to the CSD and the
IACSD and serves as a high-level focal point for promoting sustainable development throughout the United Nations.[54]

There are many activities for these various bodies to coordinate. For instance, the U.N. Development Programme—the
U.N. system's central development agency—has a key role to play
by ensuring that the activities it funds are environmentally
sound. The World Health Organization promulgates air and
water pollution guidelines that are considered the international norm; the World Meteorological Organization has made
important contributions to better understanding of the com-
plexities of climate science through its co-sponsorship of the
Intergovernmental Panel on Climate Change; and the U.N.
Food and Agriculture Organization is actively involved in pro-

moting sustainable agriculture projects and in protecting dwindling fisheries. The U.N. Fund for Population Activities (UNFPA)
provided critical leadership in the preparation for the Fall 1994
U.N. Conference on Population and Development in Cairo,
and is now active in seeing that its groundbreaking Cairo action
plan is aggressively implemented.[55]

Although Agenda 21 diplomatically reaffirms the importance of UNEP, in fact the institutional decisions made at Rio
undermined UNEP's prestige and confused its mission. The
CSD was granted both a political and a coordinating role, while
UNEP's traditional catalytic and information-gathering functions were reasserted. UNEP thus lost a mandate for a political
role, which it could in theory have played since its Governing
Council is composed of governments. And its mission to integrate environmental activities into the work of other U.N. agencies was largely usurped by shifting this responsibility to the
CSD and the IACSD. The unstated fact of the matter was that
assigning these functions to a new body was a vote of no con-
fidence in UNEP's ability to carry out these tasks effectively.[56]

Whatever its effects on the overall coherence of U.N. environmental programs, by mid-1995 the CSD had met three
times—with mixed results. On the positive side, it has provided a forum where governments and nongovernmental partici-
pants can share information about successes and failures in
implementing the Rio accords at the national and local levels.
Agenda 21 called on all nations to devise national sustainable
development strategies, and by June 1995, a total of 130 had created national organizations charged with implementing Agenda
21. However, only 17 countries have devised actual strategies
based on their deliberations, though 17 more are in the process
of doing so. There is also a growing movement worldwide to create sustainable cities and communities. The Toronto-based
International Council for Local Environmental Initiatives is
spearheading a campaign to promote the adoption of local
Agenda 21s. An estimated 1,200 cities in 33 countries—including Buga, Colombia; Quito, Ecuador; and Lahti, Finland—
already have such initiatives under way.[57]

Governments are also using the CSD to exchange views on
contentious issues that cut across traditional sectoral lines. For

instance, the commission has taken up the role of trade in sustainable development as well as the question of changing unsustainable production and consumption patterns. It is also working to encourage governments to develop and use sustainable development indicators to supplement traditional reliance on the national income accounts. At the 1995 session, governments evaluated the adequacy of existing international actions to protect biodiversity, forests, and mountains, and to combat desertification and drought. This session led to the creation of an Inter-Governmental Panel on Forests to study whether or not a new international agreement is needed to protect this resource globally. It also launched an initiative to phase out the use of lead in gasoline around the world. In addition, the 1995 session featured panel discussions on key subjects on the annual agenda, which allowed for a freer exchange of views than the formal sessions did. In 1996, the CSD will consider atmospheric and oceanic issues, among other items.[58]

Furthermore, the CSD has spurred cooperation among U.N. agencies, including the World Bank. These agencies now produce joint reports detailing their collective work in implementing the sections of Agenda 21 being reviewed in any particular year. This has proved to be a valuable coordinating mechanism.

Despite these useful initiatives, the CSD suffers from structural defects that impede substantive progress. First, its mandate is so broad that priorities are often difficult to discern. Second, the official reporting process has not worked well. Many governments do

Governments are using the CSD to exchange views on contentious issues.

not submit the required reports on national actions to implement Agenda 21. Those that do comply with this requirement tend to deliver documents that are long on self-congratulation and short on substantive analysis of remaining challenges. Finally, the CSD commands no resources of its own and has no coercive or regulatory powers, so it has no means of ensuring that its pronouncements are translated into actual policy changes at the national or local level.[59]

The result of these deficiencies is that the CSD is acquiring a reputation in some quarters as a talk shop where not much of real significance happens. If the commission is to improve its standing, it will have to hone its agenda. For instance, a high-level panel convened by the Interaction Council (an independent group consisting of former heads of government) recommended that instead of relying on national reports, the CSD should request studies by independent experts. In addition, the panel recommended that the secretariat report directly to governments and the Secretary-General on priority initiatives, rather than to the General Assembly and the Economic and Social Council. Other procedural reforms could also help improve the CSD's effectiveness. For instance, the U.S.-based National Wildlife Federation, on behalf of a coalition of NGOs, proposes that the ministerial-level segment of the CSD's annual session occur before rather than after the regular deliberations, in order to enable follow-through on initiatives endorsed by the ministers.[60]

Meanwhile, yet another institution has emerged as a major contender for recognition as the most significant U.N. agency in the environmental arena—the United Nations Development Programme. In 1993, Gus Speth, the former head of the Washington, D.C.-based World Resources Institute, took over the helm of UNDP. Speth has strong environmental credentials and has moved aggressively to try to transform UNDP into an agency that promotes people-centered, environmentally sustainable development. In 1993, UNDP spent some $470 million on environmentally related programs—more than a quarter of its total resources that year.[61]

UNDP was entrusted by governments in Rio with promoting "capacity building" for sustainable development. This means helping countries design sustainable development policies and strengthen the domestic institutions required to implement them. For this purpose, governments have donated $50 million to a special UNDP fund for a program called Capacity 21, which now has projects under way in 30 countries. For instance, Capacity 21 is helping China to develop a domestic-level Agenda 21 that will guide both national policies and international assistance, and it is assisting Lebanon in incorporating environmental management principles into the country's national reconstruction program. Another innovative program is UNDP's Sustainable Development Network, which was created in 1990 to link sources and users of information on sustainable development around the world through a computer network.[62]

In early 1995, UNDP created a new Sustainable Energy and Environment Division. It merged several pre-existing initiatives and expanded upon them. The new division includes units devoted to capacity building, energy and atmosphere projects, the GEF, natural resources management, and desertification. Among other things, it seeks to infuse a concern for environmentally sound development throughout UNDP's programs. In addition, sustainable development advisers have been placed in UNDP's field offices in 41 countries to help coordinate sustainable development activities at the ground level.[63]

In the U.N., a sizable gap remains between rhetoric and reality.

Although the establishment of significant environmental programs at several U.N. agencies is a promising development, a sizable gap remains between rhetoric and reality. Many of the agencies that now trumpet their environmental programs, including FAO and UNDP, have been criticized in the past for promoting environmentally insensitive development projects. And not all of the criticism belongs to the past. A recent independent review of the implementation of UNDP's environmental management guidelines commissioned by the agency itself concluded that many of its country offices commonly disregard them. Pressure is also beginning to build from outside to hold UNDP to its word on sustainable development. For instance, the International Rivers Network has found fault with UNDP (among many other bilateral and multilateral donors) for its support of the Mekong River Committee and the commission that has succeeded it in Southeast Asia, which—with little opportunity for public input—have facilitated an agreement that activists fear will pave the way for the construction of several new dams on the river without adequate assessment of their environmental and social impacts.[64]

Greening the Bretton Woods Institutions

In addition to playing a key role in managing the international economy, the Bretton Woods institutions—the World Bank, the International Monetary Fund, and the new World Trade Organization—potentially can make an important contribution to the effort to secure a sustainable future. Because the global economy and the natural resource base that supports it are inextricably linked, environmental issues merit a prominent place on the agendas of these bodies. A major challenge in the years to come is to reform them so that they support, rather than undermine, sustainable development.

Reorienting the World Bank's lending program is a particularly important priority, because its size ($20.8 billion in 1994 alone) makes it a dominant source of development financing and gives it a singularly powerful voice on policy matters. The Bank exerts influence in the countries to which it makes loans both through the projects it chooses to finance and by the conditions it places on how the money is to be spent. All too often, however, this influence has been negative, with the Bank funding debacles such as large hydroelectric dams and coal-fired power plants that have wrought ecological havoc and led to the relocation of millions of people. In one infamous case, for example, World Bank support for the Polonoroeste regional development scheme of road building and agricultural settlement in the Brazilian state of Rondonia contributed to rapid deforestation of the area during the 1980s; by one estimate, the share of the state that had been denuded increased from 1.7 percent to 16.1 percent between 1978 and 1991.[65]

Since the Bank first came under intense environmental scrutiny in the mid-eighties, it has taken steps to polish its tarnished image. In 1987, then President Barber Conable announced several measures aimed at making environmentally sound development a greater priority throughout the Bank's lending program. They included the creation of a central environmental department and environmental units in each regional bureau and the requirement of environmental impact assessments for all loans. Over the ensuing years, the Bank has promulgated a number of new policies to point its lending in a more ecologi-

cally and socially sound direction, including policies on indige-
nous peoples, the power sector, forestry lending, and the resettlement of displaced peoples. In 1993, the Bank created a new
vice-presidency for Environmentally Sustainable Development
with responsibility for three departments: environment; agriculture and natural resources; and transportation, water, and
urban development.[66]

Besides better policies on paper, there have been some signs
of real change in the Bank's lending program. For instance, the
amount of money devoted to free-standing environmental loans
has increased. In 1994, the Bank committed $2.4 billion for 25
projects specifically designed to protect natural resources and
improve environmental quality. This amounted to a more than
30-fold rise in such spending since 1989, though critics charge
that much of the increase can be accounted for by changes in the
type of project counted as "environmental." In addition, the
Bank has worked to increase lending for education, population,
health, and nutrition—key sectors for sustainable development.
Lending to these areas rose from 5 percent of total loans in fiscal years 1981-83 to 14 percent in 1990-92.[67]

Despite this progress, the Bank has a long way to go before
it can claim to have taken the sustainable development message to heart. Most of its investment is still devoted to loans
to governments for large infrastructure projects—despite a
growing willingness on the part of the private sector to finance
such undertakings. A 1991 study by the International Institute
for Energy Conservation (IIEC) in Washington, D.C., found
that less than 1 percent of the $45 billion loaned for energy
between 1980 and 1990 was devoted to investments in end-use
energy efficiency. Most of the rest went to large hydroelectric
and coal plants, many of which wreak enormous environmental damage. In the U.S., by contrast, demand-side management programs garnered roughly 7 percent of all utility
expenditures in 1992. Similarly in the water sector, despite
abundant evidence that small-scale alternatives to the construction of large-scale projects merit support, an analysis by
the Environmental Defense Fund (EDF) and the International
Rivers Network finds that less than 4 percent of the $35 billion
invested by the Bank in water projects over the eighties was

devoted to small-scale irrigation, water conservation, and watershed management.[68]

Another problem with the Bank's environmental record is that its forward-looking policies are often breached. Despite a new energy policy that encourages investments in end-use energy efficiency, for example, a 1994 study by EDF and the Natural Resources Defense Council (NRDC) found only two of forty-six power sector loans in the pipeline to be compatible with the new policy papers on energy. As for the Bank's resettlement policy, a 1994 internal review suggests that it is routinely violated, documenting 146 ongoing projects that together are currently displacing 2 million people.[69]

The best explanation for the gap between policy and practice at the Bank comes from within. In June 1992 an internal report written by former World Bank Vice President Willi Wapenhans concluded that the organization's projects were routinely failing to live up to its own criteria for success, such as meeting rates of return and other lending conditions. Wapenhans blamed the situation on what he called the Bank's "pervasive preoccupation with new lending."[70]

This fixation with getting money out has many sources, including the desire to infuse debt-burdened countries with cash and the tendency, typical of many large organizations, to confuse quantity with quality. For the environment, and for the people whose livelihoods depend on keeping it intact, the World Bank's "lending culture" can have catastrophic results—harmful projects proceed despite breaches of Bank policies, and countries are forced to overexploit natural resources such as timber and fisheries in order to generate the foreign exchange they need to repay the loans.[71]

If the World Bank were to promote truly sustainable development, it would place far less emphasis on large infrastructure projects that often are environmentally and socially disruptive and far more on smaller efforts carried out in close cooperation with local peoples—such as ecologically sensitive agricultural techniques or solar-powered water pumping. Lending for infrastructure would not disappear entirely, but would be refocussed. The Bank would fund fewer highways and coal-fired power plants, on the one hand, and more urban rail systems, natural gas-fired turbines for cogeneration, and sewage treatment plants, on the other. Although the institution might actually lend *less* money under this scenario, each dollar would contribute far more to the cause of sustainable development. The Bank could then devote some of the savings to providing the extra staff time required to make these smaller projects work.[72]

Another priority for the World Bank ought to be to develop policies aimed at ensuring compatibility between major environmental conventions, such as the climate and biological diversity treaties, and its lending program. This would be in keeping with a Bank policy that prevents lending in violation of international treaties, and it would help avoid developments like Bank plans for a massive investment in coal-fired power plants in India—which are expected to become collec-

The World Bank's forward-looking policies are often breached.

tively one of the single largest sources of carbon emissions in the world during the next decade. In one small step in this direction, the Bank has initiated a program that will begin to integrate global considerations into some national environmental action plans, country assistance strategies, and other documents. In addition, governments can promote greater attention to global priorities in multilateral lending through the conventions themselves. Parties to the climate convention, for example, could call for the World Bank to report on the greenhouse gas emissions expected to result from proposed projects.[73]

As the Bank contemplates its future under the leadership of a new president, James D. Wolfensohn, there are calls from many quarters for the institution to shift away from its traditional mandate to lend to governments and toward a growing role in facilitating private sector investment. This is a response to the fact that private investment is expanding rapidly in many parts of the world, calling into question the need for Bank-brokered finance in those regions. According to the Bank, private investment flows to developing countries in 1994 reached $173 billion—four times higher than in 1989 and more than eight times the total volume of World Bank lending in 1994.[74]

One way in which the Bank's involvement with the private sector is likely to increase is through an expansion of the International Finance Corporation, a World Bank arm that lends directly to private enterprises. In 1994, the IFC loaned $2.5 billion for 231 projects—16 percent of total World Bank disbursements that year. It is growing quickly and is likely to continue to expand in the years ahead. The Multilateral Investment Guarantee Agency (MIGA) is another Bank program that promotes private investment by ensuring against political risk and by other means. It, too, is likely to assume an increasingly prominent role in the years ahead.[75]

For those concerned with the environment, this shifting emphasis toward the private sector is a mixed blessing. On the one hand, both the IFC and MIGA could be used to help facilitate some of the investments in new technologies needed in the transition to a sustainable society, from hazardous-waste-minimizing production facilities to efficient compact fluorescent lightbulbs. The IFC's environmental portfolio is in fact growing fast. One promising proposal is for the IFC to channel funds through financial intermediaries to a range of small-scale, environmentally sound enterprises such as composting businesses and non-timber forest product ventures. In another new initiative, the Bank and the IFC are cooperating to establish venture capital funds to promote biodiversity investments as well as energy efficiency and renewable energy projects.[76]

On the other hand, both the IFC and MIGA also help facilitate large investment projects with worrisome environmental impacts—including dam building, oil and gas development, and mineral extraction. Both institutions are in theory bound by the Bank's environmental and social policies. But enforcement has been lax. And their actual operating procedures are sometimes different—and weaker—than those elsewhere in the Bank. Seeing that all of these far-reaching policies are indeed applied to IFC and MIGA activities would help ensure that the growing emphasis at the Bank on the private sector promotes rather than undermines environmental sustainability.[77]

Another way in which the World Bank can influence the course of private sector development is through the policy advice it provides as part of structural adjustment lending. Both the Bank and the International Monetary Fund proffer this type of loan, which involves large cash infusions that are intended to help heavily indebted countries become solvent. In return for access to this financing, both the Bank and the Fund require recipient countries to adopt "structural adjustment programs" that include a range of policy measures intended to set their economic houses in order and thus render them creditworthy. Common policy prescriptions include steep cuts in government expenditures, devaluation of currencies, and reductions in subsidies and trade barriers.[78]

The product of often difficult negotiations between Bank and IMF officials and recipient governments, structural adjustment programs have proven extremely controversial. Many development experts and Third World governments charge that the reduced subsidies and slashed governmental expenditures generally prescribed, disproportionately hurt the poor and fail to restore economic health to recipient countries.[79]

How structural adjustment programs affect the environment is a complicated question. Other things being equal, the emphasis on quickly boosting exports to earn foreign exchange could be expected to lead to the destruction of natural resources—such as forests, wetlands, and mangroves—along with the excessive development of ecologically damaging industries such as mining. Requirements that countries drastically reduce government expenditures could cause the elimination or postponement of crucial government activities, such as wildlife management or enforcement of environmental laws. Finally, to the extent that structural adjustment programs hurt the poor, they will hurt the environment as well, given the tendency for poverty and environmental degradation to go hand in hand. For instance, unemployed laborers might increasingly make their way into the tropical rainforest to engage in slash-and-burn agriculture.[80]

If, however, the Bank and the IMF were to treat environmental reform as an important element of structural adjustment, these programs could become a powerful tool for encouraging environmentally beneficial programs while still achieving their original objective of economic stabilization. Cutting subsidies to ecologically damaging industries such as mining and energy development, for instance, helps to achieve environmental, as well as economic, goals. Other policy recommendations could also have positive results for the environment. For instance, a loan agreement with Haiti pointed out that government-imposed trade barriers on imported agricultural products were having the unintended effect of aggravating soil erosion by encouraging grain production on marginal lands. Removing the barriers, as the loan agreement recommended, would produce an environmental gain.[81]

The World Bank has taken a number of steps in recent years to integrate environmental considerations into its structural adjustment operations. For instance, environmental factors are now supposed to be considered in all adjustment loans, and a paper issued in 1994 provides staff with concrete suggestions as to how best to do this. Although the report was a positive development, steps need to be taken to ensure that its advice is heeded.[82]

The IMF, however, has so far resisted all but the most elementary environmental reforms. The U.S. Congress passed a bill in 1989 directing the U.S. Treasury Department to use its influence at the Fund to promote meaningful changes, including the creation of a special unit to explore the linkages between the IMF's economic policy prescriptions and the sustainable management of natural resources, and requirements for the systemic weighing of environmental considerations as part of IMF lending agreements. So far, however, the IMF has done little more than assign three economists to do environmental research. In February 1991, the Fund's executive directors explicitly rejected the idea of creating an environment department.[83]

At the moment, any environmental benefits are merely incidental by-products of IMF policy prescriptions rather than integral goals. The staff of the Fund as well as its governing board have been reluctant to recognize that environmental health and economic prosperity are inextricably linked, and that many macroeconomic policy prescriptions affect the environment greatly. Amending the Fund's Articles of Agreement to reflect this reality would be an important step toward making the IMF better able to incorporate environmental imperatives into its programs.

Finally, the latest addition to the Bretton Woods system, the World Trade Organization, also promises to have profound environmental implications. The WTO was created in December 1993 as an outgrowth of the long-running Uruguay Round of trade negotiations under the aegis of the General Agreement on Tariffs and Trade. As part of this deal, trade ministers agreed to create a committee on trade and environment within the newly formed WTO. This committee is charged with exploring ways to ensure that trade rules and environmental goals are "mutually supportive."[84]

That environmental protection at least has a seat at the trade table is important. However, it is only a first step. Now that governments have voiced strong rhetorical support for making trade liberalization and environmental protection compatible, they face the considerable challenge of

The IMF has so far resisted all but the most elementary environmental reforms.

determining exactly how to reconcile the two goals—a challenge that will not be easily met.[85]

In the absence of policies to ensure that prices reflect their full environmental costs, trade liberalization can fuel unsustainable economic activity, including the depletion of natural resources such as timber and fisheries. It also can foster the creation of pollution havens in areas where enforcement of environmental laws is lax, as has been the case, for example, in the heavily polluted *maquiladora* zone along the U.S.-Mexico border.[86]

Furthermore, environmentalists have watched with concern as environmental laws have increasingly been challenged on grounds of violating world trade rules. For instance, Mexico and the Europen Union have each argued successfully before GATT panels that provisions of the U.S. Marine Mammal Protection Act (prohibiting imports of tuna from Mexico because the tuna was caught in a way that killed excessive numbers of dolphins) violate the agreement. Similarly, the European Union recently charged (unsuccessfully in the end) that U.S. laws

designed to promote the purchase of fuel-efficient vehicles con-
stituted a disguised trade barrier. Perhaps the biggest concern for
international environmental policymaking is that provisions
of environmental treaties calling for trade penalties as an enforcement tool will be found in violation of the WTO.[87]

Trade officials, for their part, worry that capriciously applied
environmental laws will function as trade barriers. For instance,
many developing countries are concerned that a proliferation of
eco-labelling schemes in industrial countries will keep their
products out of northern markets. Many trade officials also
worry that environmental laws can serve as cover for what are
really just commercial barriers. The challenge is to devise rules
that allow countries to pursue legitimate environmental objectives while leaving no room for camouflaged trade restrictions.
The new Uruguay Round trade rules attempted to accomplish
this. Unfortunately, they may instead have made legitimate
environmental laws vulnerable to successful challenges at the
WTO.[88]

Probably the single most important reform needed to place
world trade on a more sustainable footing is widespread inter-
nalization of environmental costs through tax policy and other
reforms. By increasing the price of coal-based electricity to
reflect the impact of its use on the atmosphere, for instance, a
tax on carbon dioxide emissions might give wind power the edge
it needs to be competitive, helping to stave off the threat of
global warming. Similarly, if wood from primary forests were
priced to reflect the loss of biological diversity suffered as a
result of its harvesting, timber from sustainably managed stands
would become more competitive in national and global markets.
Yet fears of being uncompetitive in international markets could
make it difficult for one country to promote such cost-inter-
nalizing policies without similar actions by its primary trading
partners. Determining how to overcome this hurdle will be
one of the most important challenges facing the new Committee
on Trade and Environment.[89]

Democratizing Global Environmental Governance

In theory, international treaties and institutions are compacts among sovereign nations. Individual citizens have no direct role in the international legal system. They are expected to make their voices heard through the indirect route of influencing the policies of their own national governments, thereby affecting the positions these governments advocate in international forums.[90]

Yet this theory is increasingly breaking down in practice. In fact, a range of non-state actors—including environmental groups, scientists, and the business community—now exert a direct and powerful influence in international environmental negotiations and institutions. Both the U.N. conferences and the sessions in which environmental treaties are negotiated are now routinely attended by scores of NGOs from all over the globe. International institutions such as the U.N. Commission on Sustainable Development, the Global Environment Facility, and the World Bank are the subject of intense NGO interest and scrutiny. All of them have developed elaborate procedures and processes for interacting with the non-governmental community.[91]

But despite the recent growth in interaction of NGOs with the United Nations, the relationship between the two is not an easy one. Citizens' groups working at the global level face formidable obstacles. There are no provisions for public participation comparable to those that are virtually taken for granted at the national level in democracies around the world. Nor is there anything resembling an elected parliament in the United Nations or any of its agencies. Although the U.N. has begun to experiment with occasional public hearings on topics of special concern, these continue to be rare events. No formal provisions are made for public review or comment on international treaties, nor is there a mechanism for bringing citizen suits at the World Court. International negotiations are often closed to public participation, and access to documents of critical interest to the public is generally restricted. Many NGOs resent their second-rate status within the international system, and have grown frustrated by the seemingly constant battles required to obtain what they see as the rudimentary tools essential to operating effectively.[92]

U.N. officials and government representatives, for their part, sometimes grow frustrated with NGOs. Some of the more confrontational tactics, such as Greenpeace's showering of dollar bills on the 1994 annual meeting of the World Bank, antagonize governmental officials. It also sometimes appears to them that NGOs devote endless time and energy to questions of process at the expense of substantive issues. In addition, the growing role of NGOs in international forums raises difficult issues of accountability. NGOs, unlike democratic national governments, cannot claim the legitimacy conferred by the ballot box. Their sources of legitimacy are more complex, deriving from factors such as unique knowledge or experience.[93]

And yet, despite the tensions, the growing involvement of NGOs in the United Nations is an encouraging development that is essential both for reversing global ecological decline and for restoring public legitimacy and support for this beleaguered organization.

Much of the recent NGO activity in international policy-making dates to the June 1992 Earth Summit, which was a watershed for the democratization of global environmental governance. The 20,000 concerned citizens and activists who attended the Rio conference from around the world outnumbered official representatives by at least two to one. Similarly, more than 4,000 NGOs participated in the Cairo population conference, where they were widely credited with helping to shape the terms of the debate. Some of the organizations represented at these meetings—such as Friends of the Earth, Greenpeace, the International Planned Parenthood Federation, and the World Wide Fund for Nature (WWF)—are themselves international, representing global bases of support rather than parochial national interests. They are answerable to constituencies sizable enough to rival the populations of some nation states: WWF has 3 million members and Greenpeace has 4.1 million. Taken together, all this activity adds up to the creation of a bona fide global environmental movement that stands to become as influential at the international level as it has been within countries.[94]

Working through international coalitions such as the Climate Action Network and the Women's Environment and Development Organization, these groups are a powerful force. Daily newsletters produced by citizens' organizations, including *Eco* and the *Earth Negotiations Bulletin,* have become mainstays of the international negotiating process. Widely read by official delegates and NGOs alike during international meetings, they reveal key failures in negotiations and prevent the obscure language of international diplomacy from shielding governments from accountability for their actions.[95]

> **The Earth Summit was a watershed for the democratization of global environmental governance.**

The participation of the international scientific community is also critical. International panels of scientists convened to study both ozone depletion and climate change played instrumental roles in forging the scientific consensus needed to push these political processes forward. The treaties on these two problems then created scientific advisory groups that meet regularly and offer advice on whether the agreements need to be updated in light of new scientific information.

The business community is also becoming a growing force in international environmental negotiations—for both good and ill. In a demonstration of the positive role business groups can play, U.S. industry came to support the Montreal Protocol strongly because it saw national legislation as inevitable and did not want to be at a competitive disadvantage as a result. And the Business Council for Sustainable Development, which included some 50 chief executives from the world's largest corporations, was active in the lead-up to the Earth Summit. The Council opposed language in Agenda 21 that would have advocated developing standards to regulate multinational corporations. At the same time, it argued persuasively in its report *Changing Course* that sound environmental policies and sound business practices go hand in hand.[96]

In the ongoing international climate talks, business interests have vocally weighed in on both sides of the issue. Oil and coal companies see their profits threatened by any tightening of the global warming accord, and thus they have organized themselves into a "Global Climate Coalition" that threatens to become a powerful blocking force. On the other hand, companies promoting energy efficiency, renewable energy, and natural gas stand to gain under the agreement, and they favor international action to strengthen it. They have begun to participate in international climate negotiations through the U.S.-based Business Council for a Sustainable Energy Future and a recently created European counterpart group. Insurance industries are also increasingly concerned that projected storm damage related to global warming could represent a large financial liability, and they have sent representatives to observe recent climate negotiations.[97]

International parliamentarians are another potentially powerful group of players on the global stage. The New York-based Parliamentarians for Global Action works to promote the more active involvement of parliamentarians in the U.N. The Global Legislators Organization for a Balanced Environment (GLOBE)—composed of representatives from Europe, Japan, and the United States—works cooperatively to increase pressure for action to preserve the global environment. In a similar initiative, in December 1994 an international group of legislators convened in Washington to consider ways of improving oversight of the World Bank and the International Monetary Fund.[98]

Agenda 21 encourages the democratization of international policymaking by focussing on the important role of "major groups" (including citizens' groups, labor unions, farmers, women, business interests, and others) and by endorsing the need to make information freely and widely available. In an important precedent, the Commission on Sustainable Development has based its rules for NGO participation on the liberal regulations that were in effect for the Rio conference. As a result, more than 500 groups are accredited to observe CSD deliberations and make selective interventions. An international NGO Steering Committee has recently been created to help promote collaboration among these groups and to facilitate interaction with the secretariat of the CSD as well as with governments.[99]

One interesting NGO initiative at the CSD is Earth Summit Watch, a project of the U.S.-based Natural Resources Defense Council in cooperation with several other groups. This effort has led to two reports based on in-depth surveys of actions taken to put Agenda 21 and other Rio initiatives into practice around the world. *Four in '94*, which was prepared for the 1994 CSD session, asked governments to list concrete actions taken in four portions of the agenda up for review that year—health, human settlements, fresh water, and toxic chemicals and hazardous waste. Among the findings: 38 of 72 countries surveyed have taken steps to reduce lead exposure such as moving toward lead-free gasoline; 24 are planning or constructing water treatment projects; 69 of the 178 countries at Rio have ratified the Basel convention on trade in hazardous wastes, and 74 have imposed national bans on hazardous waste imports; yet only 10 of the 72 countries surveyed have taken steps to protect rivers. For the time being, most countries are simply reporting on actions they were planning to take anyway. But over time, "peer pressure" may induce them to move forward on new policies. A *Five in '95* report is planned for this year covering timber certification, Cairo follow-up, protection of marine biodiversity hotspots, reduction of pesticide use, and promotion of environmental democracy.[100]

Another way in which NGOs participate in the Rio follow-up process is through their involvement in some national sustainable development commissions. These bodies take different forms in different countries. Some are composed only of government representatives; others are "multistakeholder" forums composed of a range of interested parties, including government, NGOs, and the business sector. In 1987, the Canadian Round Table on the Environment and the Economy pioneered the concept of bringing diverse parties to the table. This has since been widely replicated, by the Philippine Council on Sustainable Development and the President's Council on Sustainable Development in the United States, among others. Indeed, 53 countries have now launched such multistakeholder initiatives.[101]

The U.N. Economic and Social Council is currently review-ing the rules for participation of citizens' groups in the U.N. system at large. Some of those involved in the debate advocate making it easier for groups to be involved, taking the Rio expe-rience as their guide. Among other things, they urge opening up the criteria for U.N. consultative status to include more national and regional groups, expanding speaking rights, and increasing access to documents and meetings. Others resist these suggestions, worrying about the system being over-whelmed by sheer numbers, or about whether the citizens' groups are accountable to the public at large. The outcome of these deliberations on the role of NGOs at the U.N. remains to be seen, but it seems likely that the UNCED process has set a new standard for participation that the U.N. will have difficulty back-ing away from.[102]

Indeed, pressure is growing for the U.N. to take bold steps to formalize the new importance of NGOs. Some proposals envi-sion creating a new assembly within the United Nations where the views of the people of the world could be more directly represented than under the current system. One model for such an assembly is the directly elected European Parliament. A more feasible alternative might be to create a body composed of representatives of national parliaments—perhaps as a transition to a full-fledged peoples assembly. This idea has been endorsed in a number of recent reports. At a minimum, the U.N. would do well to make more regular use of public hearings.[103]

Aggressive actions are also needed at the Bretton Woods institutions to make them more open and accountable. To an even greater extent than at the U.N. itself, information and documents at these organizations are tightly guarded, and nego-tiations between governments are completely closed to observers, with no NGO newsletters offering blow-by-blow accounts of who says what to whom.

The GATT and the WTO have been subject to particular-ly strong criticism for their secretive procedures. When a national law is challenged as a trade barrier under these agreements, the case is heard behind closed doors by a panel of professors and bureaucrats steeped in the intricacies of world trade law, but not in the needs of the planet. Legal briefs and other critical information are generally unavailable to the public, and there is no opportunity for citizens' groups to testify or make submissions. Governments are currently discussing rules on public participation for the Committee on Trade and Environment of the World Trade Organization. Preliminary reports suggest that the fight for public access will be long and hard fought.[104]

Despite a checkered history regarding openness, the World Bank instituted two new policies in 1993 that others would do well to emulate. Under a new information policy, more Bank documents will be publicly available than before, and an information center has been established to disseminate them. The second change—the creation of an independent inspection panel—will provide an impartial forum where board members or private citizens can raise complaints about projects that violate the Bank's own policies, rules, and procedures. Although both initiatives were watered down in the negotiating process, they nonetheless represent important reforms. It will be up to the concerned public to test the limits of these new policies and to press for them to be strengthened—and replicated elsewhere.[105]

Some changes along similar lines are actually afoot at the notoriously secretive IMF. In 1994, a coalition of environment and development groups successfully lobbied the U.S. Congress to withhold $75 million of the Clinton Administration's appropriation request of $100 million for the IMF's Enhanced Structural Adjustment Facility pending changes at the Fund that would increase public access to its documents. And in July 1994, the Fund's directors did take modest steps in this direction.[106]

Pressure is growing for the U.N. to take bold steps to formalize the new importance of NGOs.

Besides access to information, the public needs the opportunity to become a fuller partner in the development process itself. All too often, "development" has served the purposes of a country's elite but not of its poorest members. A growing body of evidence suggests that for a project to succeed, its planning process must include the people it is supposed to benefit. In other words, aid should be demand-driven rather than imposed from above. Both UNDP and the World Bank have recently developed strategies to more systematically include citizens in developing and executing projects. The challenge, as always, will be moving from words to action.[107]

One model for moving toward this more participatory approach to development is the recent growth in the number of "environmental funds" around the world. Since 1990, at least $850 million has been committed to such entities in more than 20 countries. These small funds to finance conservation investments can take the form of trust funds, endowments, foundations, or other grant-making bodies. They receive money from diverse sources, including fees for park visits, private foundations, the Global Environment Facility, and bilateral donors. Governed by boards on which NGOs are heavily represented, local people play an important role in identifying and carrying out projects. So far, this has led to impressive results.[108]

Moving Forward

In June 1995, representatives of the United Nations, national governments, and non-governmental organizations gathered in San Francisco to mark the 50th anniversary of the signing of the U.N. Charter. Although this event was a celebration of what the United Nations had achieved in its first half century, it was also an occasion for sober reflection about some of the organization's limitations. This anniversary year is most appropriately viewed less as a birthday party for the U.N. than as a launching pad for far-reaching reforms to ensure that it can respond to the demands that will be made of it over the next 50 years.

As these deliberations continue in the months and years ahead, the need to upgrade the U.N.'s environmental machinery merits a prominent place on the agenda. The United Nations has responded to the emergence of environmental issues as a third pillar of international relations alongside economic and security affairs by helping to develop hundreds of international-al agreements and by launching active environmental programs. As encouraging as this growing involvement of many different United Nations bodies in environmental matters is, however, the price of success has been a measure of duplication and ineffi-ciency. Rather than a cohesive system for the environment, what we have is a patchwork quilt. This disorganized system needs to be streamlined if it is to become capable of reversing global ecological decline.

The idea that the U.N.'s environmental capacities need to be strengthened is not a new one. In the years prior to the Earth Summit, a number of proposals appeared. Perhaps the most ambitious one is the Declaration of the Hague, a call in 1989 by 17 heads of state from countries as varied as Brazil, France, India, Japan, West Germany, and Zimbabwe for the creation of a new or newly strengthened environmental institution within the U.N. endowed with considerable law-making and enforce-ment powers. Another proposal, advocated at times by Norway, the Soviet Union, and the United Kingdom, is to set up an envi-ronmental security council. A third idea is to give the task of managing the global commons to the Trusteeship Council, orig-inally created to assist countries with decolonization and now in need of a new mission. This idea was recently endorsed by the Commission on Global Governance, a high-level independent commission chaired by Ingvar Carlsson, the Prime Minister of Sweden, and Shridath Ramphal, former Secretary-General of the British Commonwealth. In another recent proposal, Daniel Esty of Yale University has suggested the creation of a Global Environmental Organization (GEO) to, among other things, develop basic environmental principles analogous to widely recognized trade principles such as "most-favored-nation" status and "nondiscrimination."[109]

Before launching into any new reforms, however, it is impor-tant to recognize that the institutional initiatives launched at the Earth Summit have already had some modest success. The cre-ation of the Commission on Sustainable Development, in par-ticular, helped boost the prominence of the environment throughout the far-flung U.N. system by creating a high-level political forum where these issues can be considered at U.N.

headquarters in New York. The fact remains, however, that there is no full-fledged environment agency within the U.N. system. The U.N.'s 50th anniversary would be an opportune time to fill this gap.

Some will argue now—as they did when UNEP was created in 1972—that establishing a strong environment agency would take pressure off the other U.N. agencies to integrate environmental considerations into their programs. But the need for such integration exists at the national level as well, and experience suggests that the existence of strong domestic environment agencies has promoted rather than discouraged it. Elder statesman George Kennan had it right in 1970, when he wrote the following appeal for the establishment of an international environmental agency in an article that appeared in *Foreign Affairs* two years before the Stockholm conference:

> There is a considerable body of opinion, particularly in U.N. circles, to the effect that it is a mistake to separate the function of conservation and protection of natural resources from that of the development and exploitation of these resources for productive purposes. According to this view, there should not be separate organizations concerned with conservation. Considerations of an environmental nature should rather be built from the outset into all those activities that are concerned with the productive exploitation of natural resources, so that environmental needs would be met, so to speak, at the source. This writer must respectfully disagree....What is needed here is a watchdog; and the conscience and sense of duty of the watchdog must not be confused by contrary duties and undertakings.[110]

Twenty-five years later, it is time to fulfill Kennan's vision by transforming UNEP into an operational U.N. Environment Agency, that is, one that has a mandate to undertake actual projects. In setting up such a body, it would be important to ensure that it consolidates, and not merely supplements, existing environmental efforts. For instance, in addition to most of

UNEP's functions, some of the tasks now performed by UNDP's environmental unit could be subsumed into the new body, as well as most of the responsibilities now belonging to the secretariats for the conventions and the GEF. Close links would need to be established with the Commission on Sustainable Development and the Bretton Woods Institutions. To be effective, the new agency would need to have sizable funds at its disposal and be centrally located—in either New York or Geneva.

Because the Commission on Sustainable Development is already providing a political forum, the new agency would instead concentrate on programs. For instance, it could play a critical role by serving as an information gatherer and clearing-house—as UNEP already does on a small scale. Such an organization might also serve as the executing agency for some UNDP-financed projects. For instance, just as WHO and FAO collaborate with UNDP on the ground, an environment agency could be a partner in recycling or land reclamation projects. It might also run programs providing information about environmentally sound technologies, and give advice about effective environmental policymaking and institution-building. Many of these activities could be undertaken through a decentralized network of regional field offices.[111]

It is time to transform UNEP into an operational U.N. Environment Agency.

To the extent the new agency does take on a negotiating role, it would likely involve the elaboration of some common minimum international environmental standards, particularly for industries such as paper manufacturing, in which pollution control costs are high enough to affect international competitiveness. The organization could also serve as an umbrella organization for the current scattered collection of treaty bodies—just as the domestic environment agencies oversee the implementation of national environmental laws. This could improve the opportunities for bargaining and facilitate access for nongovernmental groups.[112]

A precedent is provided by the International Labour Organisation (ILO), which constantly modifies and strengthens the hundreds of standards it has issued on concerns such as workplace safety and child labor. The ILO also reviews whether members are complying with its standards and provides countries with technical assistance to help them with this task. It often generates enough pressure in a first, investigatory stage to bring an errant country into line, making its second stage—a public hearing to explain delinquency—unnecessary. Representatives from both management and labor actually form part of the governing body of the ILO, through a unique tripartite system in which they share equal standing with governments. The World Intellectual Property Organization, which has helped rationalize the many complex and often overlapping international agreements in this domain, is another relevant model.[113]

Besides creating an improved institutional structure for ongoing international environmental efforts, it is important to ensure a secure funding base. And yet, at the same time that celebrations of the U.N.'s 50th birthday are taking place, governments are contemplating draconian funding cuts. This is despite the fact that the investments governments make in international institutions are cost-effective, and pale in comparison to spending in other areas. For instance, the entire U.S. international affairs budget amounts to just one percent of the total federal budget, and contributions to international organizations represent only a small fraction of this total. When averaged out across the U.S. population, the entire annual U.S. contribution to the U.N. comes to just $7 per person—about the cost of a single movie ticket. In the United States, the Clinton Administration has requested that Congress appropriate just $16 million for UNEP for FY1996—a proposal Congress is likely to slash. Meanwhile, the U.S. intelligence budget is estimated at $28 billion—almost two-thousand times as much.[114]

In view of the continued problems with securing national contributions to the U.N., governments need to create some form of dedicated funding mechanism to finance the investments required for the transition to a sustainable society—including environmental programs, social initiatives, and peacekeeping efforts. Among the possibilities for such a fund are a levy on carbon emissions, on international air travel, or perhaps on

international flows of money. To discourage currency specula-
tion, Nobel-laureate James Tobin has suggested that a 0.5-percent
tax be placed on foreign-exchange transactions, which Tobin cal-
culates would have the side-benefit of raising more than $1.5 tril-
lion annually. But even a far smaller levy would raise sizable
funds. For instance a tax of just 0.05 percent on current daily
currency transactions would raise $150 billion annually—more
than 75 times the recent replenishment of GEF.[115]

Surveys indicate that most people would support substan-
tially increasing the U.N.'s authority in global environmental
matters. A 1993 Gallup Survey found that public concern about
environmental problems is high around the world—dispelling
the myth that only rich countries can
afford to care about these issues. In
the Philippines, 94 percent of those **The investments**
polled said they cared about environ-
mental problems a "great deal" or a **governments**
"fair amount"; in Nigeria, 87 percent **make in**
responded in the same way, as did 85
percent and 66 percent respectively of **international**
those people questioned in the United **institutions are**
States and in Japan. Support for inter- **cost-effective.**
national cooperation to solve shared
problems was also high: majorities in
both industrial and developing countries favor giving an international environmental agency both financial resources and
substantial clout.[116]

Yet despite public support for far-reaching changes, the international response to the threat of ecological collapse remains seri-
ously inadequate. Fifty years ago, with large parts of Europe and
Asia devastated by World War II, the world community
embarked on an impressive period of institution-building that
set the tone for the next half-century. Now a similar burst of
innovation is needed to forge a new global partnership that
can enable the world to meet the daunting environmental challenges that are expected in the next millennium.

Notes

1. Clyde H. Farnsworth, "Canada and Spain Face Off Over Fish Rights," *New York Times*, March 12, 1995; Charles Petit, "New Hints of Global Warming," *San Francisco Chronicle*, April 17, 1995; "The Climate Time Bomb: Signs of Climate Change from the Greenpeace Database," Update Summary, Climate Summit, March 1995; David Brown, "Ebola Virus: A Mystery With A Deadly Plot," *Washington Post*, May 30, 1995; Laurie Garrett, *The Coming Plague* (New York: Farrar, Straus and Giroux, 1994).

2. Office of Public Information, United Nations, New York, "Charter of the United Nations and Statute of the International Court of Justice."

3. Stettinius quoted in "United Nations-Bretton Woods Collaboration: How Much is Enough?," Report of the Twenty-Sixth United Nations Issues Conference, Sponsored by the Stanley Foundation, February 24-26, 1995; for a discussion of the history of relations between the Bretton Woods institutions and the rest of the United Nations system, see Erskine Childers with Brian Urquhart, *Renewing the United Nations System* (Uppsala, Sweden: Dag Hammarkjöld Foundation, 1994). For general background on the United Nations system, see United Nations, *Everyone's United Nations* (New York: U.N. Department of Public Information, June 1986 —Tenth Edition). The U.N.'s 14 specialized agencies are rather autonomous from the rest of the U.N. system, with the precise relationship defined by special agreements. In this paper, the term United Nations will be used broadly to refer to the U.N.'s political organs in New York and all of its affiliated agencies, including the Bretton Woods institutions.

4. "Environmental Damage Robs Countries' Income," *World Bank News*, March 25, 1993, based on David Pearce and Jeremy Warford, *World Without End* (Washington, D.C.: World Bank, 1993); "Airborne Pollution May be Hurting Eskimo Health," *Multinational Environmental Outlook*, January 5, 1989.

5. Thomas F. Homer-Dixon, "Environmental Scarcities and Violent Conflict: Evidence from Cases," *International Security*, Summer 1994.

6. For a description of Swiss efforts to develop an accord covering migratory birds in the 1870s, see Lynton K. Caldwell, "Beyond Environmental Diplomacy: The Changing Institutional Structure of International Cooperation," in John E. Carroll, ed., *International Environmental Diplomacy* (New York: Cambridge University Press, 1988); for a discussion of the Stockholm Conference and its aftermath, see Lynton Keith Caldwell, *International Environmental Policy* (Durham, N.C.: Duke University Press, 1990).

7. Michael Grubb et al., *The Earth Summit Agreements: A Guide and Assessment* (London: Earthscan Publications Ltd., 1993); United Nations Framework Convention on Climate Change and Convention on Biological Diversity included in Lakshman D. Guruswamy, Sir Geoffrey W. R. Palmer, and Burns H. Weston, *International Environmental Law and World Order*, Supplement of Basic Documents (St. Paul, Minn.: West Publishing Co., 1994).

8. Grubb et al., op. cit. note 7; United Nations, *Agenda 21: The United Nations Program of Action From Rio* (New York: U.N. Publications, 1992).

9. Carbon Dioxide Information Analysis Center, *Trends '93: A Compendium of Data on Global Change* (Oak Ridge, Tenn., 1994); David Malin Roodman, "Carbon Emissions Rise," in Lester R. Brown, Nicholas Lenssen, and Hal Kane, *Vital Signs 1995* (New York: W.W. Norton & Co., 1995); L.R. Oldeman, V.W.P van Engelen, and J.H.M. Pulles, "The Extent of Human-Induced Soil Degradation," Annex 5 of L.R. Holdeman, R.T.A. Hakkeling, and W.G. Sombroek, *World Map of the Status of Human-Induced Soil Degradation: An Explanatory Note*, rev. 2d ed. (Wageningen, The Netherlands: International Soil Reference and Information Centre, 1990); other trends documented and discussed in World Resources Institute, *World Resources 1992-93* (New York: Oxford University Press, 1992).

10. Hilary F. French, "Making Environmental Treaties Work," *Scientific American*, December 1994; Ronald B. Mitchell, "Compliance with International Treaties: Lessons from Intentional Oil Pollution," *Environment*, May 1995.

11. John Tierney, "Earthly Worries Supplant Euphoria of Moon Shots," *New York Times*, July 20, 1994.

12. Figure 1 based on U.N. Environment Programme (UNEP), *Register of International Treaties and Other Agreements in the Field of the Environment 1993* (Nairobi: 1993) and Mark Labelle, UN Treaty Office, New York, private communication, June 4, 1995; Edith Brown-Weiss, Paul Szasz, and Daniel Magraw, *International Environment Law: Basic Instruments and References* (Irvington-on-Hudson, N.Y.: Transnational Publishers, Inc., 1992).

13. Marc Levy, "European Acid Rain: The Power of Tote-Board Diplomacy," *Institutions for the Earth: Sources of Effective International Environmental Protection* (Cambridge, Mass.: MIT Press, 1993); Megan Ryan, "CFC Production Plummeting," in Brown, Lenssen, and Kane, op. cit. note 9; "Africa's Elephants Could Soon Be Under the Gun Again," *Christian Science Monitor*, February 2, 1992; Gareth Porter and Janet Welsh Brown, *Global Environmental Politics* (Boulder, Colo.: Westview Press, 1991).

14. Table 1 is based on the following sources: Guruswamy, Palmer, and Weston, op. cit. note 7; U.S. General Accounting Office (GAO), *International Environment: International Agreements Are Not Well Monitored* (Washington, D.C.: January 1992); "Whale Conservation," U.S. Congressional Research Service, August 30, 1990; Ray Gambell, International Whaling Commission, London, private communication, October 11, 1994; Porter and Brown, op. cit. note 13; IUCN-World Conservation Union, *The Law of the Sea: Priorities and Responsibilities in Implementing the Convention* (Gland: 1995); Elliott A. Norse, ed., *Global Marine Biological Diversity* (Washington, D.C.: Island Press, 1993); "Africa's Elephants Could Soon Be Under the Gun Again," op.cit. note 13; Ryan, op. cit. note 13; UNEP, "Historic Agreement Reached Between OECD and Non-OECD Countries to Ban Export of Hazardous Wastes," Press Release, March 28, 1994; "Concrete Action on Protocol Deferred; Two-year Negotiation Process Launched," *International Environment Reporter*, April 19, 1995; and "More Than 100 Countries Agree On International Desertification Treaty," *International Environment Reporter*, June 29, 1994. Number of parties from Mark Labelle, U.N. Treaty Office, New York, private communication, June 7, 1995; Wilma Wilson, Treaty Office, Department of State, Washington, D.C., private communication, June 20, 1995; Holly Reed, TRAFFIC, World Wildlife Fund, Washington, D.C., private communication, June 28, 1995; Linda Young, Legal Division, International Maritime Organization, London, private communication, June 20, 1995; and Madhava Sarma, ozone secretariat, Nairobi, Kenya, private communication, June 27, 1995.

15. Canute James, "Oceans Set to Yield Up Their Treasures," *Financial Times*, July 7, 1994; Rebecca Fowler, "Law of the Sea: An Odyssey to U.S. Acceptance," *Washington Post*, July 29, 1994; ratification information from "Environmental/ Conservation Community Statement in Support of U.S. Accession to the LOS Convention," June 8, 1995.

16. Peter Weber, *Abandoned Seas: Reversing the Decline of the Oceans*, Worldwatch Paper 116 (Washington, D.C.: Worldwatch Institute, November 1993); *The Law of the Sea: United Nations Convention on the Law of the Sea* (New York: United Nations, 1983); "Environmental/Conservation Community Statement," op. cit. note 15.

17. Weber, op. cit. note 16; "Environmental/Conservation Community Statement," op. cit. note 15.

18. Michael A. Jacobson, "The United Nations' Regional Seas Programme: How Does It Measure Up?" *Coastal Management*, Vol. 23, 1995; Peter M. Haas, *Saving the Mediterranean* (New York: Columbia University Press, 1990); "UNEP Tackles Freshwater, Coastal and Marine Pollution," UNEP Information Note, May 19, 1995.

19. Food and Agriculture Organization data provided in Peter Weber, *Net Loss: Fish, Jobs, and the Marine Environment*, Worldwatch Paper 120 (Washington, D.C.: Worldwatch Institute, July 1994); "Summary of the Third Session of the UN Conference on Straddling Fish Stocks and Highly Migratory Fish Stocks 15-26 August 1994," *Earth Negotiations Bulletin*, August 29, 1994.

20. "Summary of the Third Session of the UN Conference," op. cit. note 19; Clyde H. Farnsworth, "North Atlantic Fishing Pact Could Become World Model," *New York Times*, April 17, 1995; Anne Swardson, "Fish Accord Could Save Many Species," *Washington Post*, April 18, 1995; David Balton, U.S. Department of State, remarks to the American Society of International Law, Washington, D.C., June 13, 1995.

21. Richard Elliot Benedick, *Ozone Diplomacy* (Cambridge, Mass.: Harvard University Press, 1991); Douglas G. Cogan, *Stones in a Glass House* (Washington, D.C.: Investor Responsibility Research Center, 1988).

22. Montreal Protocol and subsequent amendments from Guruswamy, Palmer, and Weston, op. cit. note 7; UNEP, "Copenhagen Amendment on Ozone Layer to Enter Into Force," Press Release, Nairobi, March 22, 1994; UNEP, "Ozone Treaty Experts Make Significant Progress on Drafting Possible Adjustments and Amendments to Montreal Protocol," Press Release, Nairobi, May 17, 1995; "Montreal Protocol Working Group Puts Off New Proposals Until November," *International Environment Reporter*, May 17, 1995.

23. As of June 1995, 149 countries had ratified the Montreal Protocol, from Sarma, op. cit. note 14; UNEP, "Copenhagen Amendment," op. cit. note 22; UNEP, World Meteorological Organization, U.S. National Aeronautics and Space

Administration, and National Oceanic and Atmospheric Administration, "Scientific Assessment of Ozone Depletion: 1994," Executive Summary, Washington, D.C., August 19, 1994; UNEP, "The 1994 Science, Environmental Effects, and Technology and Economic Assessments," Synthesis Report, December 29, 1994. Figure 2 based on data supplied by Michael Prather and Mack McFarland, E.I. Du Pont de Nemours, private communication, March 18, 1994. The figure uses measured data through 1991 and projections thereafter. The top curve assumes continued growth of 3 percent per year. The next assumes continued compliance with the original Montreal Protocol, with 3 percent growth of ozone-depleting substances not controlled by the agreement. The third assumes compliance with the London agreements, with HCFC phaseout by 2040. The bottom curve assumes compliance with the Copenhagen agreements.

24. "Climate Change Treaty Comes into Force," *International Environment Reporter*, March 23, 1994; ratification information from Mark Labelle, op. cit. note 14.

25. U.N. Convention on Climate Change, in Guruswamy, Palmer, and Weston, op. cit. note 7.

26. International Energy Agency (IEA), *Climate Change Policy Initiatives—1994 Update, Vol. 1, OECD Countries* (Paris: Organisation for Economic Co-operation and Development (OECD), 1994); "IEA Reviews Energy Policies in Germany, UK, and Denmark," *Energy, Economics, and Climate Change*, August 1994; Christopher Flavin and Odil Tunali, "Getting Warmer: Looking For a Way Out of the Climate Impasse," *World Watch*, March/April 1995.

27. "EU Ratifies Climate Convention Without Carbon/Energy Tax," *Energy, Economics, and Climate Change*, December 1993; IEA, *Energy Prices and Taxes: 1994*, Second Quarter (Paris: OECD, 1994); United States Climate Action Network and Climate Network Europe, "Independent NGO Evaluations of National Plans for Climate Change Mitigation: OECD Countries," *Third Review*, January 1995; Climate Action Network—Central and Eastern Europe and Climate Network Europe, "Independent NGO Evaluations of National Plans for Climate Change Mitigation: Central and Eastern Europe," *First Review*, January 1995; Flavin and Tunali, op. cit. note 26; IEA, *World Energy Outlook, 1995 Edition* (Paris: OECD, 1995).

28. Executive Summary, "Draft Summary for Policymakers of the 1994 Working Group I Report on Radiative Forcing of Climate Change," Intergovernmental Panel on Climate Change (IPCC), Maastricht, The Netherlands, September 15, 1994; IPCC, *Climate Change: The IPCC Scientific Assessment* (New York: Cambridge University Press, 1990); U.S. Climate Action Network, Letter to the Hon. Timothy E. Wirth, U.S. Undersecretary of State for Global Affairs, July 28, 1994; "Small Island Nations Protocol Proposes 20 Percent CO_2 Cut for Developed Nations," *International Environment Reporter*, October 5, 1994; Christopher Flavin, "Climate Policy: Showdown in Berlin," *World Watch*, July/August 1995; "Concrete Action on Protocol Deferred, op. cit. note 14.

29. David E. Pitt, "Biological Pact Passes Into Law," *New York Times*, January 2, 1994; ratifications from Labelle, op. cit. note 14; "UNEP Head Calls Meeting Successful; Cites Significant Progress on Many Issues," *International Environment*

Reporter, December 14, 1994; "Congress Fails to Ratify Treaty to Protect World's Biological Diversity," *International Environment Reporter*, October 19, 1994.

30. Jessica Mathews, "Rights to Life," *Washington Post*, April 24, 1994; Walter V. Reid, Vice President, World Resources Institute, Hearings on Convention on Biological Diversity, Committee on Foreign Relations, U.S. Senate, Washington, D.C., April 12, 1992.

31. Reid, op. cit. note 30; World Resources Institute (WRI), World Conservation Union, and UNEP, "Global Biodiversity Strategy: Policy-makers' Guide," Washington, D.C., 1992.

32. Walter V. Reid et al., eds., *Biodiversity Prospecting: Using Genetic Resources for Sustainable Development* (Washington, D.C.: WRI, 1993).

33. Steven M. Lanou, World Resources Institute, "National Biodiversity Planning Activities: Overview," unpublished matrix, Washington, D.C., June 7, 1994; World Resources Institute, *World Resources 1994-95* (New York: Oxford University Press, 1994).

34. Françoise Burhenne-Guilmin and Susan Casey-Lefkowitz, "The New Law of Biodiversity," *Yearbook of International Environmental Law 1992* (Boston/Dordrecht: Graham & Trotman/Martinus Nijhoff, 1993); "UNEP Head Calls Meeting Successful," op. cit. note 29.

35. GAO, op. cit. note 14. The U.S. E.P.A.'s air office, for instance, had a budget of $564 million in 1995, per Congressional Green Sheets, *Environment and Energy Special Report*, February 8, 1995.

36. Scott Hajost and Quinlan J. Shea, "An Overview of Enforcement and Compliance Mechanisms in International Environmental Agreements," presented to International Enforcement Workshop, Utrecht, The Netherlands, May 8-10, 1990; Gordon Binder and Jonathan Adams, "Does CITES Need More Teeth," *Conservation Issues*, World Wildlife Fund, Washington, D.C., October 1994.

37. GAO, op. cit. note 14.

38. Ibid.; "Concrete Action on Protocol Deferred," op. cit. note 14; "UNEP Selected as Permanent Secretariat For Treaty But Location Still Unresolved," *International Environment Reporter*, December 14, 1995; United Nations, *Agenda 21*, op. cit. note 8; Rosemary Sandford, "International Environmental Treaty Secretariats: Stage-Hands or Actors?" in Helge Ole Bergesen and Georg Parmann, Eds., *Green Globe Yearbook 1994* (Oxford: Oxford University Press, 1994).

39. "International Ban Imposed on Thai Wildlife Trade," *The Nation* (Bangkok), April 16, 1991; "Government Will Not Oppose U.S. Ban on Thai Wildlife Imports," *The Nation* (Bangkok), July 5, 1991; "Does CITES Need More Teeth?" op. cit. note 36; Rosalind Twum-Barima and Laura B. Campbell, *Protecting the Ozone Layer through Trade Measures: Reconciling the Trade Provisions of the Montreal Protocol and the rules of the GATT*, UNEP Environment and Trade Series 6, UNEP, Geneva, 1994; "Uruguay Round Ministerial Decision on Trade and Environment," Marrakesh, April 14, 1994.

40. Alexander Wood, "The Multilateral Fund for the Implementation of the

Montreal Protocol," *International Environmental Affairs*, Fall 1993; UNEP, "Draft Report of the Fifth Meeting of the Parties to the Montreal Protocol on Substances that Deplete the Ozone Layer," Bangkok, November 17-19, 1993.

41. "Montreal Protocol Working Group," op. cit. note 22; Speech by Ms. Elizabeth Dowdeswell, Executive Director, UNEP, at the Opening of the Eleventh Meeting of the Open-Ended Working Group of the Parties to the Montreal Protocol, Nairobi, May 8, 1995.

42. Global Environment Facility (GEF), brochure, Washington, D.C., December 1991; Conventions on biological diversity and on climate change from Guruswamy, Palmer, and Weston, op. cit. note 7; Seth Dunn, "The Berlin Climate Change Summit: Implications for International Environmental Law," *International Environment Reporter*, May 31, 1995; "Global Environment Facility To Continue as 'Interim' Financing Source for Projects," *International Environment Reporter*, December 14, 1994; "Agreement Reached on Funding GEF; Program to Receive More than $2 Billion," *International Environment Reporter*, March 23, 1994; GEF, "Instrument for the Establishment of the Restructured Global Environment Facility," Report of the GEF Participants Meeting, Geneva, Switzerland, March 14-16, 1994; GEF, "Quarterly Operational Report," Washington, D.C., April 1995. Countries eligible for ozone project funding under the Interim Multilateral Fund are ineligible for GEF support for this purpose. The main beneficiaries of GEF support for ozone projects are countries from the former Soviet Union and Eastern Europe.

43. GEF, brochure, op. cit. note 42.

44. "The Southern Green Fund: Views from the South on the Global Environment Facility," World Wide Fund for Nature-International (WWF-International), Gland, Switzerland, undated; Bruce Rich, *Mortgaging the Earth: The World Bank, Environmental Impoverishment, and the Crisis of Development* (Boston: Beacon Press, 1994); United Nations Development Program (UNDP), UNEP, and World Bank, *Global Environment Facility: Independent Evaluation of the Pilot Phase* (Washington, D.C.: World Bank, 1994).

45. GEF, "Instrument for the Establishment of the Restructured Global Environment Facility," op. cit. note 42.

46. GEF, "Draft Operational Strategy," prepared for GEF Council Meeting, Washington, D.C., July 18-20, 1995; "Joint Summary of the Chairs," GEF Council Meeting, Global Environment Facility, May 3-5, 1995.

47. Amanda Wolf with David Reed, *Incremental Cost Analysis in Addressing Global Environmental Problems* (Washington, D.C.: World Wide Fund for Nature-International (WWF-International) June 1994); Ian A. Bowles and Glenn T. Prickett, *Reframing the Green Window* (Washington, D.C.: Conservation International and Natural Resources Defense Council (NRDC), 1994); UNDP, UNEP, and World Bank, op. cit. note 44; "Joint Summary of the Chairs," op. cit. note 46.

48. Bowles and Prickett, op. cit. note 47; UNDP, UNEP, and World Bank, op. cit. note 44; David Reed, ed., *The Global Environment Facility: Sharing Responsibility for the Biosphere* (Washington, D.C.: WWF International Institutions Policy

Program, undated).

49. Konrad von Moltke, "Why UNEP Matters," A Report for World Wide Fund for Nature International, March 1995; UNEP, "UNEP: Two Decades of Achievement and Challenge," Nairobi, October 1992; Peter S. Thacher, "Global Security and Risk Management: Background to Institutional Options for Management of the Global Environment and Commons," World Federation of United Nations Associations, 1991.

50. UNEP, *Twenty Years Since Stockholm*, 1992 Annual Report of the Executive Director (Nairobi: 1993); UNDP, "Heading for Change: UNDP 1993 Annual Report," New York, undated; von Moltke, op. cit. note 49; National Wildlife Federation, *1993 Annual Report* (Washington, D.C.: 1993).

51. von Moltke, op. cit. note 49.

52. UNEP, op. cit. note 50; "Dowdeswell Cites 'Critical Need' for UNEP to Forge Strategic Alliances," *International Environment Reporter*, November 16, 1994; "UNEP Announces Senior Staff Appointments," *UNEP Industry and Environment*, April-June 1994.

53. Kathryn G. Sessions, "Institutionalizing the Earth Summit," UNA-USA Occasional Paper, United Nations Association of the United States of America (UNA-USA), Washington, D.C., October 1992.

54. Lee A. Kimball, "International Institutional Developments," in *Yearbook of International Law 1993* (Oxford: Oxford University Press, 1994); Lee A. Kimball, "International Institutional Developments: The U.N. Conference on Environment and Development," in *Yearbook of International Law 1992*, op. cit. note 34.

55. On the World Health Organization's (WHO) standard-setting role, see, for instance, WHO, *Air Quality Guidelines for Europe* (Copenhagen: 1987).

56. United Nations, *Agenda 21*, op. cit. note 8; von Moltke, op. cit. note 49.

57. Earth Council, NRDC, and WRI, "Directory of National Commissions on Sustainable Development," Washington, D.C., May 1994; Earth Summit Watch, *Four in '94. Assessing National Actions to Implement Agenda 21: A Country-by-Country Report* (Washington, D.C.: 1994); Diomar Silveira, Earth Council, San José, Costa Rica, private communication, June 29, 1995; Kathleen Gildred and Sheila Kelly, Citizens Network for Sustainable Development, "Sustainable Communities Working Group Paper," unpublished, July 21, 1994; "Local Agenda 21 Network News," International Council for Local Environmental Initiatives, Toronto, June 1994; Charlene Easton, International Council for Local Environmental Initiatives, private communication, June 30, 1995.

58. Martin Khor, "CSD Still Alive, But Not Yet Kicking Into Action," *Third World Economics*, June 1-15, 1994; United Nations Department for Policy Coordination and Sustainable Development, "Provisional Implementation Plan for Work Programme on Indicators of Sustainable Development," draft, June 7, 1995; "Summary of the Third Session of the UN Commission on Sustainable Development 11-28 April 1995," *Earth Negotiations Bulletin*, May 1, 1995; "U.N. Creates Special Panel to Weigh Need for Forestry Convention," and "Language Adopted by U.N. Commission Seeks Worldwide Phase-Out of Leaded Gas,"

International Environment Reporter, May 3, 1995.

59. Interaction Council, Report on the Conclusions and Recommendations by a High-level Group on "The Future Role of the Global Multilateral Organizations," The Hague, The Netherlands, May 7-8, 1994; "Reporting System on Environmental Progress Needs Simplification, Groups Tell CSD Session," *International Environment Reporter*, June 1, 1994.

60. Interaction Council, op. cit. note 59; CAPE 21/Citizens Network for Sustainable Development, Procedural Recommendations to Klaus Töpfer, Chairman of the Commission on Sustainable Development, October 1994; Barbara Bramble, "CSD Needs a Better Structure," Newsletter of the Citizens Network for Sustainable Development, Bolinas, Calif., Summer 1994.

61. James Gustave Speth, Administrator, UNDP, "With a Soul and a Vision: A New Approach to Development and a New UNDP," Address to the UNDP Staff, United Nations Secretariat, July 27, 1993; "Building a New UNDP: Agenda for Change," Presentation by James Gustave Speth, Administrator, to the UNDP Executive Board, February 17, 1994; Louis, etc., June 27, 1995; UNDP, op. cit. note 50.

62. Louis Gomez-Echeverri, UNDP, private communication, May 30, 1995; UNDP "Synopsis of Capacity 21 Programmes," brochure; Susan Becker, UNDP, private communication, June 16, 1995.

63. Becker, op. cit. note 62; Gomez-Echeverri, op. cit. note 62.

64. Nicholas Hildyard, "Sustaining the Hunger Machine: A Critique of FAO's Sustainable Agriculture and Rural Development Strategy," *The Ecologist*, November-December 1991; Konrad von Moltke and Ginny Eckert, "The United Nations Development Programme and the Environment: A Nongovernmental Assessment," WWF-International, May 1992; Lex Brown, Mabingue Ngom, and Eunice M. Shankland, "Independent Review of the UNDP Environmental Management Guidelines Training," prepared for Sustainable Energy and Environmental Division, UNDP, February 1995; "Mekong Report," *World Rivers Review*, Fourth Quarter 1994; "Mekong Agreement Signed," and "High Priority for Hydro on Mekong," *World Rivers Review*, May 1995.

65. World Bank, *Annual Report 1994* (Washington, D.C.: 1994); Rich, op. cit. note 44.

66. Address of Barber B. Conable, President, World Bank and International Finance Corporation, to WRI, Washington, D.C., May 5, 1987; World Bank, *Making Development Sustainable: The World Bank Group and the Environment Fiscal 1994* (Washington, D.C.: 1994); World Bank, *The World Bank and the Environment: Fiscal 1993* (Washington, D.C.: 1993).

67. World Bank, *Making Development Sustainable*, op. cit. note 66; World Bank, *The World Bank and the Environment: Fiscal 1993*, op. cit. note 66; World Bank, *Implementing the World Bank's Strategy to Reduce Poverty: Progress and Challenges* (Washington, D.C.: 1993).

68. World Bank, op. cit. note 65. On the private sector role in financing infrastructure, see testimony by Linda F. Powers, Enron Development Corporation,

before the Committee on Appropriations, Subcommittee on Foreign Operations, U.S. House of Representatives, January 31, 1995. Michael Philips, *The Least Cost Energy Path For Developing Countries: Energy Efficient Investments for the Multilateral Development Banks* (Washington D.C.: International Institute for Energy Conservation, 1991); U.S. expenditures on demand-side management are a Worldwatch Institute estimate based on Edison Electric Institute, *Statistical Yearbook of the Electric Utility Industry 1992* (Washington D.C.: 1993); and on Thomas Devlin, Science Applications International Corp., Arlington, Va., private communication, June 15, 1993; Leonard Sklar, International Rivers Network, and Deborah Moore and Mafruza Khan, Environmental Defense Fund (EDF), "The World Bank and its Water Policy," *Bankcheck* (International Rivers Network), January 1994.

69. NRDC, *Power Failure: A Review of the World Bank's Implementation of Its New Energy Policy* (Washington, D.C.: 1994); World Bank, *Resettlement and Development: The Bankwide Review of Projects Involving Involuntary Resettlement 1986-1993* (Washington, D.C.: 1994).

70. Portfolio Management Task Force, "Effective Implementation: Key to Development Impact," World Bank, Washington, D.C., November 3, 1992.

71. Rich, op. cit. note 44; Frances F. Korten, "The High Costs of Environmental Loans," *Asia Pacific Issues* (East-West Center), September 1993.

72. For a more detailed discussion of needed changes at the World Bank, see Hilary F. French, "Rebuilding the World Bank," in Lester R. Brown et al., *State of the World 1994* (New York: W.W. Norton & Co., 1994).

73. Greenpeace International, "Lending for the Climate: MDBs and the Climate Convention," Prepared for the 10th Session of the Intergovernmental Negotiating Committee for a Framework Convention on Climate Change," Geneva, Switzerland, August 22-September 2, 1994; Global Environment Operations, World Bank, "Business Plan: Fiscal Year 1995," Washington, D.C., 1994; Jens Rosebrock, World Bank, Washington, D.C., private communication, October 20, 1994; Liz Barratt-Brown, Kando Velasco, and Scott Hajost, "Financial Reform and the Climate Convention," *Eco* (NGO Newsletter), Climate Negotiations, Geneva, September 2, 1994.

74. Richard W. Richardson and Jonas H. Haralz, *Moving to the Market: The World Bank in Transition* (Washington, D.C.: Overseas Development Council, 1995); Bretton Woods Commission, "Bretton Woods: Looking Toward the Future," Washington, D.C., July 1994; Paul Lewis, "New World Bank: Consultant to Third World Investors," *New York Times*, April 27, 1995; investment numbers cited in "What's Ahead for the World Bank," Interviews on the Bank's Role in Promoting Sustainable Development, Charles Stewart Mott Foundation, Flint, Mich., undated.

75. World Bank, op. cit. note 65.

76. World Bank, *Making Development Sustainable*, op. cit. note 66.

77. Friends of the Earth International, "Cutting Corners: the IFC and Sustainable Development," Amsterdam, September 1994; World Bank, *Making Development Sustainable,* op. cit. note 66; Ronald Anderson, International Finance Corporation,

Washington, D.C., private communication, June 29, 1995.

78. David Reed, ed., *Structural Adjustment and the Environment* (Boulder, Colo.: Westview Press, 1992); "The IMF and the World Bank: Two Pillars of Wisdom," *The Economist*, October 12, 1991.

79. Giovanni Andrea Cornia, Richard Jolly, and Frances Stewart, eds., *Adjustment With a Human Face* (New York: Oxford University Press, 1989). More recent critiques of the effects of structural adjustment lending on the poor have been undertaken by both the International Labor Organization and the International Fund for Agricultural Development. Both are cited in Carol Capps, Church World Service and Lutheran World Relief, "The International Development Association: Flawed but Essential," statement before the Subcommittee on International Development, Finance, Trade, and Monetary Policy and the Banking Committee, U.S. House of Representatives, Washington D.C., May 5, 1993; Oxfam Policy Department, *A Case for Reform: Fifty Years of the IMF and World Bank* (Oxford: 1995).

80. Pearce and Warford, op. cit. note 4; Reed, op. cit. note 78; Wilfred and Cruz and Robert Repetto, *The Environmental Effects of Stabilization and Structural Adjustment Programs: The Philippines Case* (Washington D.C.: World Resources Institute, 1992).

81. David Pearce et al., "Debt and the Environment," *Scientific American*, June 1995; Raymond F. Mikesell & Lawrence F. Williams, *International Banks and the Environment: From Growth to Sustainability—An Unfinished Agenda* (San Francisco: Sierra Club Books, April 1992).

82. World Bank, *Making Development Sustainable*, op. cit. note 66; Mohan Munisinghe and Wilfrido Cruz, *Economywide Policies and the Environment: Lessons from Experience* (Washington, D.C.: World Bank, 1995).

83. Marijke Torfs and Jim Barnes, Friends of the Earth, unpublished memorandum, September 4, 1991.

84. "Uruguay Round Ministerial Decision on Trade and Environment," op. cit. note 39.

85. NRDC and Foundation for International Environmental Law and Development, "Environmental Priorities for the World Trading System: Recommendations to the WTO Committee on Trade and Environment," Washington, D.C., and London, 1995.

86. Hilary F. French, *Costly Tradeoffs: Reconciling Trade and the Environment*, Worldwatch Paper 113 (Washington, D.C.: Worldwatch Institute, March 1993).

87. Steve Charnovitz, "Green Roots, Bad Pruning: GATT Rules and their Application to Environmental Trade Measures," *Tulane Environmental Law Journal*, Summer 1994; Steve Charnovitz, "Dolphins and Tuna: An Analysis of the Second GATT Panel Report," *Environmental Law Reporter*, October 1994; Steve Charnovitz, "The GATT Panel Decision on Automobile Taxes," *International Environment Reporter*, November 2, 1994.

88. Daniel C. Esty, *Greening the GATT* (Washington, D.C.: Institute for International Economics, 1994); Steve Charnovitz, "The World Trade

Organization and Environmental Supervision," *International Environment Reporter*, January 26, 1994.

89. French, op. cit. note 86.

90. Werner Levi, *Contemporary International Law: A Concise Introduction* (Boulder, Col.: Westview Press, 1991).

91. Peter J. Spiro, "New Global Communities: Nongovernmental Organizations in International Decisionmaking Institutions," *Washington Quarterly*, Winter 1995.

92. David A. Wirth, "A Matchmaker's Challenge: Marrying International Law and American Environmental Law," *Virginia Journal of International Law*, Winter 1992; Daniel J. Shepard, "UN Seeks Experts' Testimony in Series of Extraordinary Hearings on Development," *Earth Times*, June 15, 1994; Pamela Leonard and Walter Hoffman, *Effective Global Environmental Protection: World Federalist Proposals to Strengthen the Role of the United Nations* (Washington, D.C.: World Federalist Association, 1990).

93. "The Annual Meeting of the IMF and World Bank," *News and Notices*, International Financial Institutions Accountability Project, Bread for the World Institute, Silver Spring, Md., November 14, 1994.

94. Lester M. Salamon, "The Rise of the Nonprofit Sector," *Foreign Affairs*, July/August 1994; Don Hinrichsen, "The Earth Summit," *The Amicus Journal*, Winter 1992; Kate Randolph, Coordinator, NGO Planning Committee for International Conference on Population and Development, private communication, October 18, 1994; Spiro, op. cit. note 91.

95. *Eco* is produced regularly by NGOs at major international negotiations. The *Earth Negotiations Bulletin* is published by the International Institute for Sustainable Development of Winnipeg, Manitoba.

96. Benedick, op. cit. note 21; Harris Gleckman, "Transnational Corporations' Strategic Responses to Sustainable Development," in Helge ole Bergesen and Georg Parmann, eds., *Green Globe Yearbook 1995* (Oxford: Oxford University Press, 1995); Stephan Schmidheiny with the Business Council for Sustainable Development, *Changing Course* (Cambridge, Mass.: The MIT Press, 1992).

97. "High Priest of the Carbon Club," translation of excerpts from *Der Spiegel* article about the Global Climate Coalition, Vol. 14, April 1995; "Constructive Industry Hits INC 10," *Eco*, Climate Negotiations, Geneva, August 26, 1994; Dorte Bernhardt, "Business Leaders Go Green," *Eco*, Climate Negotiations, Berlin, March 31, 1995; Christopher Flavin, "Industry Split Widens," *Eco*, Climate Negotiations, Berlin, April 4, 1995; Haig Simonian, "Bankers Join Greenpeace to Urge Action Over Global Warming Threat," *Financial Times*, March 27, 1995.

98. "Parliamentarians for Global Action," brochure; "Global Legislators Organization for a Balanced Environment," Activity Report, 103rd Congress; "Meeting of Multinational Group of Parliamentarians Involved in Oversight of the IMF and the World Bank," *News and Notices*, International Financial Institution Accountability Project, Bread for the World Institute, Silver Spring, Md., December 19, 1994.

99. United Nations, *Agenda 21,* op. cit. note 8; Kathryn G. Sessions, "Options for NGO Participation in the Commission on Sustainable Development," UNA-USA Background Paper, Washington, D.C., May 1993; Ferita Ayoub, Chief of NGO Section, Department of Policy Coordination and Sustainable Development, United Nations, New York, private communication, August 24, 1994; "The NGO Steering Committee to the Commission on Sustainable Development," memorandum, New York, June 5, 1994.

100. Earth Summit Watch, op. cit. note 57; "1995 Earth Summit Watch Survey," unpublished memorandum.

101. Earth Summit Watch, op. cit. note 57; Earth Council, NRDC, and WRI, op. cit. note 57; Silveira, op. cit. note 57.

102. "Key Issues for the Open-Ended Working Group on the Review of Arrangements for Consultation with Non-Governmental Organizations," Submitted by an Ad Hoc Committee of NGOs, June 23, 1994; Yolanda Kakabadse Ni with Sarah Burns, "Movers and Shapers: NGOs in International Affairs," *International Perspectives on Sustainability,* WRI, Washington, D.C., May 1994; Stanley Foundation, "The UN System and NGOs: New Relationships for a New Era?" Report of the Twenty-Fifth United Nations Issues Conference, Harriman, N.Y., February 18-20, 1994; Laurie S. Wiseberg, "Consultative Status Review Stalled," *Tribune des Droits Humains,* juin/juil. 1995.

103. Commission on Global Governance, *Our Global Neighborhood* (Oxford: Oxford University Press, 1995); Childers with Urquhart, op. cit. note 3.

104. For a discussion of the GATT dispute resolution procedure, see Charnovitz, "Dolphins and Tuna," op. cit. note 87; John Zarocostas, "Environmental Proposal for WTO Met Coolly," *Journal of Commerce,* September 19, 1994; James Cameron and Ross Ramsay, "Participation by Non-Governmental Organisations in the World Trade Organisation," Global Environment and Trade Study, undated.

105. "The World Bank Policy on Disclosure of Information," World Bank, Washington, D.C., March 1994; "Operations Inspection Function: Objectives, Mandate and Operating Procedures for an Independent Inspection Panel," World Bank, 1993; David Hunter and Lori Udall, "The World Bank's New Inspection Panel: Will It Increase the Bank's Accountability?" Center for International Environmental Law, Brief No. 1, Washington, D.C., April 1994; Barbara Bramble, "World Bank Reforms: The Beginnings of Accountability," Newsletter of the Citizens Network for Sustainable Development, Bolinas, Calif., October/November 1993.

106. Friends of the Earth, "The IMF: Why the Secrecy?," unpublished statement; Conference Report to Accompany H.R. 4426, Making Appropriations for the Foreign Operations, Export Financing, and Related Programs for the Fiscal Year Ending September 30, 1995, 103d Congress, U.S. House of Representatives, August 1, 1994.

107. Importance of participatory approaches to project success from Operations Evaluation Department, *Evaluation Results for 1991* (Washington, D.C.: World Bank, 1993), and from Bhuvan Bhatnagar and Aubrey C. Williams, eds., *Participatory Development and the World Bank: Potential Directions for Change*

(Washington, D.C.: World Bank, 1992); Jo Marie Griesgraber, ed., *Rethinking Bretton Woods: Toward Equitable, Sustainable, and Participatory Development* (Washington, D.C.: Center of Concern, 1994); UNDP, "UNDP and Organizations of Civil Society," prepared for the public events marking the 50th anniversary of the UN Charter, San Francisco, June 1995; World Bank, "The World Bank and Participation," Report to the Board of the World Bank, August 25, 1994, including NGO Addendum.

108. UNDP/GEF, "Environmental Funds: The First Five Years," A Preliminary Analysis for the OECD/DAC Working Party on Development Assistance and the Environment, April 1995; Mark Dillenbeck, IUCN-US, Washington, D.C., "National Environmental Funds: A New Mechanism for Conservation Finance," May 20, 1994.

109. Hague Declaration included in Guruswamy, Palmer, and Weston, op. cit. note 7; Patricia A. Bliss-Guest, U.S. Council on Environmental Quality, "Proposals for Institutional Reform of the UN System to Promote Sustainable Development Policies," presented at Twentieth American Bar Association Conference on the Environment, Warrenton, Va., May 18, 1991; Commission on Global Governance, op.cit. note 103; Daniel C. Esty, "GATTing the Greens," *Foreign Affairs*, November/December 1993; Daniel C. Esty, "The Case for a Global Environmental Organization," in Peter B. Kenen, ed., *Managing the World Economy: Fifty Years After Bretton Woods* (Washington, D.C.: Institute for International Economics, 1994).

110. George F. Kennan, "To Prevent a World Wasteland," *Foreign Affairs*, April 1970.

111. Branislav Gosovic, *The Quest for World Environmental Cooperation* (London and New York: Routledge, 1992); UNDP, op. cit. note 50.

112. Esty, "The Case for a Global Environmental Organization," op. cit. note 109; Gareth Porter, "Multilateral Agreement on Minimum Standards for Manufacturing and Processing Industries," Environmental and Energy Study Institute, Washington, D.C., July 1994; French, op. cit. note 10.

113. James Avery Joyce, *World Labor Rights and Their Protection* (London: Croom Helm, 1980); Steve Charnovitz, "Improving Environmental and Trade Governance," *International Environmental Affairs*, Winter 1995; Esty, "Case for a Global Environmental Organization," op. cit. note 109.

114. Frances Williams, "UN agencies 'under threat' from US cuts," *Financial Times*, May 30, 1995; Energy and Environmental Study Institute, "U.S. Development Assistance: A Visual Briefing," Washington, D.C., April 1995; "Contributions to International Organizations, International Conferences, and Contingencies," Statement of Douglas J. Bennet, Assistant Secretary of State, before the House Subcommittee on Appropriations for Commerce, Justice, State, the Judiciary and Related Agencies, March 23, 1995; "Proposed International Organizations' Voluntary Contributions, FY 1996 Request," *Washington Weekly Report*, UNA-USA, March 10, 1995; intelligence budget estimate from John Pike, Federation of American Scientists, private communication, June 13, 1995.

115. Childers with Urquhart, op. cit. note 3; UNDP, *Human Development Report*

1994 (New York: Oxford University Press, 1994).

116. Riley E. Dunlop, George H. Gallup, Jr., and Alec M. Gallup, *Health of the Planet: A George H. Gallup Memorial Survey* (Princeton, N.J.: The George H. Gallup International Institute, 1993).

PUBLICATION ORDER FORM

No. of
Copies

_____ **Total Copies**

☐ **Single Copy: $5.00**

☐ **Bulk Copies (any combination of titles)**
  ☐ 2–5: $4.00 ea. ☐ 6–20: $3.00 ea. ☐ 21 or more: $2.00 ea.
  Call Director of Communication at (202) 452-1999 for discounts on larger orders.

☐ **Membership in the Worldwatch Library: $30.00 (international airmail $45.00)**
  The paperback edition of our 250-page "annual physical of the planet,"
  State of the World, plus all Worldwatch Papers released during the calendar year.

☐ **Worldwatch Database Disk Subscription: One year for $89**
Includes current global agricultural, energy, economic, environmental, social, and military indicators from all current Worldwatch publications. Includes a mid-year update, and *Vital Signs* and *State of the World* as they are published. Can be used with Lotus 1-2-3, Quattro Pro, Excel, SuperCalc and many other spreadsheets.
Check one: _____high-density IBM-compatible or _____Macintosh

---

☐ **Subscription to *World Watch* magazine: $20.00 (international airmail $35.00)**
  Stay abreast of global environmental trends and issues with our award-winning, eminently readable bimonthly magazine.

Please include $3 postage and handling for non-subscription orders.

Make check payable to Worldwatch Institute
1776 Massachusetts Avenue, N.W., Washington, D.C. 20036-1904 USA

Enclosed is my check for U.S. $_____

VISA ☐   Mastercard ☐ _____
                                  Card Number   Expiration Date

_____
name   **daytime phone #**

_____
address

_____
city   **state**   **zip/country**   WWI

PUBLICATION ORDER FORM

No. of
Copies

_____ 57. **Nuclear Power: The Market Test** by Christopher Flavin.

_____ 58. **Air Pollution, Acid Rain, and the Future of Forests** by Sandra Postel.

_____ 60. **Soil Erosion: Quiet Crisis in the World Economy** by Lester R. Brown and
Edward C. Wolf.

_____ 61. **Electricity's Future: The Shift to Efficiency and Small-Scale Power**
by Christopher Flavin.

_____ 63. **Energy Productivity: Key to Environmental Protection and Economic Progress**
by William U. Chandler.

_____ 65. **Reversing Africa's Decline** by Lester R. Brown and Edward C. Wolf.

_____ 66. **World Oil: Coping With the Dangers of Success** by Christopher Flavin.

_____ 68. **Banishing Tobacco** by William U. Chandler.

_____ 70. **Electricity For A Developing World: New Directions** by Christopher Flavin.

_____ 71. **Altering the Earth's Chemistry: Assessing the Risks** by Sandra Postel.

_____ 75. **Reassessing Nuclear Power: The Fallout From Chernobyl** by Christopher Flavin.

_____ 77. **The Future of Urbanization: Facing the Ecological and Economic Constraints**
by Lester R. Brown and Jodi L. Jacobson.

_____ 78. **On the Brink of Extinction: Conserving The Diversity of Life** by Edward C. Wolf.

_____ 79. **Defusing the Toxics Threat: Controlling Pesticides and Industrial Waste**
by Sandra Postel.

_____ 80. **Planning the Global Family** by Jodi L. Jacobson.

_____ 81. **Renewable Energy: Today's Contribution, Tomorrow's Promise** by
Cynthia Pollock Shea.

_____ 82. **Building on Success: The Age of Energy Efficiency** by Christopher Flavin
and Alan B. Durning.

_____ 83. **Reforesting the Earth** by Sandra Postel and Lori Heise.

_____ 84. **Rethinking the Role of the Automobile** by Michael Renner.

_____ 86. **Environmental Refugees: A Yardstick of Habitability** by Jodi L. Jacobson.

_____ 88. **Action at the Grassroots: Fighting Poverty and Environmental Decline**
by Alan B. Durning.

_____ 89. **National Security: The Economic and Environmental Dimensions** by Michael Renner.

_____ 90. **The Bicycle: Vehicle for a Small Planet** by Marcia D. Lowe.

_____ 91. **Slowing Global Warming: A Worldwide Strategy** by Christopher Flavin

_____ 92. **Poverty and the Environment: Reversing the Downward Spiral** by Alan B. Durning.

_____ 93. **Water for Agriculture: Facing the Limits** by Sandra Postel.

_____ 94. **Clearing the Air: A Global Agenda** by Hilary F. French.

_____ 95. **Apartheid's Environmental Toll** by Alan B. Durning.

_____ 96. **Swords Into Plowshares: Converting to a Peace Economy** by Michael Renner.

_____ 97. **The Global Politics of Abortion** by Jodi L. Jacobson.

_____ 98. **Alternatives to the Automobile: Transport for Livable Cities** by Marcia D. Lowe.

_____ 99. **Green Revolutions: Environmental Reconstruction in Eastern Europe and the
Soviet Union** by Hilary F. French.

_____100. **Beyond the Petroleum Age: Designing a Solar Economy** by Christopher Flavin
and Nicholas Lenssen.

_____101. **Discarding the Throwaway Society** by John E. Young.

_____102. **Women's Reproductive Health: The Silent Emergency** by Jodi L. Jacobson.

_____103. **Taking Stock: Animal Farming and the Environment** by Alan B. Durning and
Holly B. Brough.

_____104. **Jobs in a Sustainable Economy** by Michael Renner.

_____105. **Shaping Cities: The Environmental and Human Dimensions** by Marcia D. Lowe.

_____106. **Nuclear Waste: The Problem That Won't Go Away** by Nicholas Lenssen.

_____107. **After the Earth Summit: The Future of Environmental Governance**
by Hilary F. French.

_____108. **Life Support: Conserving Biological Diversity** by John C. Ryan.

_____ **Total Copies**

☐ **Single Copy: $5.00**

☐ **Bulk Copies (any combination of titles)**
    ☐ 2–5: $4.00 ea.   ☐ 6–20: $3.00 ea.   ☐ 21 or more: $2.00 ea.
    Call Director of Communication at (202) 452-1999 for discounts on larger orders.

☐ **Membership in the Worldwatch Library: $30.00 (international airmail $45.00)**
    The paperback edition of our 250-page "annual physical of the planet,"
    State of the World, plus all Worldwatch Papers released during the calendar year.

☐ **Worldwatch Database Disk Subscription: One year for $89**
Includes current global agricultural, energy, economic, environmental, social, and military indicators from all current Worldwatch publications. Includes a mid-year update, and *Vital Signs* and *State of the World* as they are published. Can be used with Lotus 1-2-3, Quattro Pro, Excel, SuperCalc and many other spreadsheets.
Check one: _____high-density IBM-compatible or _____Macintosh

---

☐ **Subscription to *World Watch* magazine: $20.00 (international airmail $35.00)**
    Stay abreast of global environmental trends and issues with our award-winning,
    eminently readable bimonthly magazine.

Please include $3 postage and handling for non-subscription orders.

Make check payable to Worldwatch Institute
1776 Massachusetts Avenue, N.W., Washington, D.C. 20036-1904 USA

Enclosed is my check for U.S. $_____

VISA ☐   Mastercard ☐ _____
                      Card Number   Expiration Date

name   **daytime phone #**

address

city   **state**   **zip/country**   WWP